GRATEFUL & GROUNDED KIDS

Raising Responsible, Tech-Wise, and Money-Smart Children in an Age of Entitlement

DOUG GOODMUNDSON

Grateful & Grounded Kids:
Raising Responsible, Tech-Wise, and Money-Smart Children in an Age of Entitlement
By Doug Goodmundson

Copyright © 2026 by Doug Goodmundson

Published by Rich Road Resources
Bloomington, Minnesota, USA
RichRoadStewardship.com

ISBN 979-8-9956275-0-0 (print)

All rights reserved. No part of this publication may be reproduced, distributed, stored in a retrieval system, or transmitted in any form or by any means—electronic, mechanical, photocopying, recording, scanning, or otherwise—without prior written permission of the author, except for brief quotations used in reviews, articles, or teaching settings with proper attribution.

The views expressed in this book are those of the author and are not intended as legal, financial, or technological advice. Readers are encouraged to seek qualified professional counsel regarding specific financial or legal decisions. Names, examples, and scenarios may be composites or used illustratively to teach principles of biblical stewardship, responsibility, and wise decision-making.

All Scripture quotations, unless otherwise indicated, are from the New King James Version®. Copyright © 1982 by Thomas Nelson. Used by permission. All rights reserved. Scripture quotations marked NIV are from the Holy Bible, New International Version®, NIV®. Copyright ©1973, 1978, 1984, 2011 by Biblica, Inc.™ Used by permission of Zondervan. All rights reserved worldwide. www.zondervan.com. The "NIV" and "New International Version" are trademarks registered in the United States Patent and Trademark Office by Biblica, Inc.™ Scripture quotations marked ESV are from the ESV® Bible (The Holy Bible, English Standard Version®), copyright © 2001 by Crossway, a publishing ministry of Good News Publishers. ESV Text Edition: 2025. The ESV text may not be quoted in any publication made available to the public by a Creative Commons license. The ESV may not be translated in whole or in part into any other language. Used by permission. All rights reserved.

Cover and interior by Rich Road Resources
Editing by Avodah Editorial Services

Printed in the United States of America
26 27 28 29 30 5 4 3 2

Contents

Introduction

I did not write this book as a one-stop solution to every issue it raises—though if it helps you take meaningful steps, that's a win.

My deeper aim is to name the dilemma many parents feel, offer time-tested wisdom to address it, and lay out the framework we've found helpful in our own home, while making space for the kind of conversation where this model can be thoughtfully applied in real communities.

This approach rises or falls on context. It is built on principles, not rules—and principles take time to interpret well. Every home is different.

This book grew out of years of teaching in churches, schools, and parent networks, as well as ongoing conversations with families navigating childhood in a rapidly changing world. What I've learned along the way is that while principles can be written down, formation is always lived out in real homes—with real children and real constraints.

Because of that, these ideas tend to take root best through conversation and in community. This book and its accompanying resources are meant to provide a clear framework and shared language for thinking about stewardship in the home. But for many families, the real progress comes when these ideas are explored together in community.

If you find yourself wanting to put a thoughtful plan in place for your family, I encourage you to consider gathering a small group of parents to work through these ideas together. Or, many families will invite me to share this material through individual sessions or workshops in their churches, schools, or parent networks.

If this framework would be helpful for your community I would welcome the opportunity to explore doing so with yours. My hope is that this book serves as a starting point—not an endpoint—for thoughtful, contextual, and life-giving conversation.

I also want to say that beginning with just one of the three topics of emphasis I share about in this book is a great way to get started. If you have questions or I can be of assistance, you can find information on my website at www.RichRoadStewardship.com or reach out to me at doug@richroadstewardship.com.

—Doug

Part 1

Why a Grounded Home Matters

Before we talk about systems, plans, or strategies, we need to understand the deeper forces shaping life inside our homes.

Every family develops a culture. Sometimes it is intentional, but often it forms quietly through habits, expectations, and the environment children grow up within. Over time, that culture shapes how children understand privilege, responsibility, gratitude, and work.

In recent generations, many families have experienced unprecedented levels of comfort and opportunity. While these are blessings, they also introduce new challenges. When privilege grows faster than responsibility, children can begin to develop habits of entitlement that quietly erode resilience and relationships.

The chapters in this section explore the ideas behind a grounded home—how culture forms, how entitlement develops, and why responsibility plays such a critical role in shaping healthy families.

Before we can build practical plans, we first need to understand the foundation.

Chapter 1

A Household Economy for Kids

You would think that someone who has spent fifteen years teaching and talking about stewardship—financially, biblically, practically—would have this figured out at home.

I thought I did. I didn't.

For most of my adult life, stewardship has been a central thread of my work and calling. I've spent years helping churches, nonprofits, families, and individuals think carefully about money, work, and generosity. I've taught on it, preached it, written about it, and coached others through it. Stewardship has shaped how I understand faith and formation, and what it means for me to live well: loving God and loving my neighbor.

By trade, I am a financial advisor. My day-to-day work involves helping people and companies build their financial realities around their values. Given all of that, I assumed this experience would translate naturally into our home. But a few years ago, something began to feel off—particularly as our kids started getting older. At the time, my wife and I had four children, ages four, six, eight, and twelve.

Everything began to feel like an uphill battle—which didn't make sense, because by most measures, life was getting easier. We were past the diapers, getting closer to being out of the car seat stage, and our oldest was old enough to babysit so we could get out for an evening.

But attitudes were on the struggle bus. The demand for screen time was relentless and never enough. Chores and basic responsibility felt harder than they should have been. None of this was dramatic, but it was constant. To be sure, most of the families we are in connection with felt similarly. In other words, this wasn't unique to us.

Let me ask you a question: *Do you feel great about how your kids interact with technology in your home, and great about how they interact with responsibility like chores and contributing to the home?* Most of the parents I'm talking to, virtually all of them, would say they do not feel great about either of these.

Our kids had an absolutely great life. But their attitudes reflected otherwise, and it felt less like immaturity and more like entitlement. The steady stream of requests for more was wearing me down. Resistance to responsibility and chores wasn't helping. Nothing ever seemed to satisfy. Everything felt out of balance.

And then there was technology, God bless it. Wasn't technology supposed to make our lives easier? Because that was not the case for us. I found myself functioning as the family's unofficial IT manager, trying to keep up while my kids pushed for more—more access, more screen time, more freedom. It was exhausting, often frustrating, and rarely felt simple or intuitive. Technology was making my job as a parent harder, especially when it came to shaping my kids' character and understanding. And that mattered deeply to me. Here we were, married for eighteen years and raising four kids, and life was amazing and simultaneously harder than it felt like it should have been.

Is this just the new normal? I thought.

The Moment That Changed Everything

And then one morning a couple of years ago, I went a little further during my usual time of prayer and journaling before the kids were awake. Sitting there, I felt the same as I had for a while. Tired. A bit discouraged. Even a little hopeless.

So I closed my eyes and began to imagine the future. A Thanksgiving dinner, years down the road. Fifteen years out. All of us gathered around the table. I pictured my oldest son sitting directly across from me. At the time, he was on the verge of becoming a teenager. In my imagination, he was twenty-seven—the same age I was when he was born.

Who would he be? What kind of man would he have become? Would he still love hockey? Would he be responsible? Married? Would he love God? Would he be happy?

At first, the picture brought a sense of gladness. It was good to think about. But then I let myself consider a different outcome. What if things didn't turn out well? What if he struggled to launch out in life? What if he resisted responsibility, drifted from relationships, or refused to listen to guidance? Would he still be reachable? Would he trust me? Would our relationship still be intact?

More than anything, I realized what I wanted was a relationship that was healthy and could last the test of time. The problem was, we had started triggering each other. I felt like his expectations were often exaggerated or unrealistic, and when I addressed something that hadn't been done the way we had agreed, his response was rarely simple. Sometimes it turned into an argument. Other times, he would roll his eyes or mutter something under his breath as he walked away. For a dad, that kind of response can be enough to light a fuse.

I felt like I was up against something I couldn't quite name. *Are my kids spoiled? We're not rich . . . or are we? Do they actually have too much?* How would I even know if this was real, or just a phase like so many parents say it is? From the outside, I don't think most people would've called our home out of control. But it felt that way to me. And more than that, it didn't feel like something they were simply going to grow out of, at least not without a lot of unnecessary conflict along the way.

The Relationship Between Privilege and Entitlement

We are raising children in the most privileged environment of abundance in human history.[1,2] That is not a complaint. It is simply a reality. Our kids have access to comfort, opportunity, entertainment, safety, and technology that previous generations could not have imagined. Much of this privilege is good. Some of it is wonderful. Much of it we are grateful for.

But privilege is never neutral. Privilege tends to breed either gratitude or entitlement. And the difference is often the presence or absence of structure and responsibility. Not just responsibility for personal pursuits (sports, activities, homework), but responsibility for the community around them, the home they live in, and the family they belong to.

Scripture repeatedly warns that abundance carries risk. In Deuteronomy 8, Moses cautions God's people that after years of wandering in the wilderness—learning to trust God and fighting to secure their land—the real danger would come later. When they finally settle in the Promised Land, when they have eaten and are satisfied, when their homes are secure and their resources multiply, the greatest threat will not be scarcity but abundance—and the temptation to forget the Lord.

That morning, I was reminded of a book I had read years earlier, *The Opposite of Spoiled* by Ron Lieber. I pulled it off the shelf and began flipping through the pages, looking for how he defined what it actually means for a child to be "spoiled." Here's how he explains it:

> Spoiled children tend to have four primary things in common, though they don't all have to present at once: they have few chores or other responsibilities, there aren't many rules that govern their behavior or schedules, parents and others lavish them with time and assistance, and they have a lot of material possessions. It doesn't have to cost all that much to spoil a child. In fact, three of the four factors in my definition of spoiled don't cost a thing.[3]

Yup, that made sense. When I thought about what an entitled or spoiled person looked like, it seemed probable that my kids were already drifting in that direction. In theory, we valued responsibility, structure, accountability, and giving our kids opportunities to fail and grow. In practice, however, we were not living that out very well. Good old ordinary responsibility in the home had fallen behind in importance to, well, almost everything. Sports, family events, playing with friends, video games, homework, the list went on.

To be honest, I had started to feel frustrated with my kids themselves, as if they had somehow allowed this entitlement to take root. Like they should have known better. Like they had done something to me, and now I was holding it against them.

Then the puzzle pieces started coming together for me. The more I sat with that thought, the more I realized how absurd it was. Kids do not spoil themselves. Parents do.

If my kids were becoming entitled, it was not their fault. It was our fault as parents. That realization brought a kind of clarity I hadn't had before. This was not complicated. It was not gray. They were not responsible for what had been shaped in them. We as parents were. And as uncomfortable as that was to admit, it finally gave me a clear place to start.

Then another reality came into focus. Entitlement does not appear overnight. It forms gradually when two things consistently exist together:

an abundance of privilege and a lack of real responsibility and structure. That understanding led to a simple but powerful insight: **Entitlement grows when privilege outpaces responsibility**.

Many of the concerns I had for my kids were not just cultural or generational, though those influences are real. They were being shaped, in large part, by the environment I was creating and the culture of our home.

Another realization followed close behind. **Entitlement does not just affect behavior; it also erodes relationships**. If the relationship I hoped to have with my kids, both now and in the future, was going to be healthy and meaningful, then this was something I needed to address while they were still under my roof.

Because entitlement is not something people simply grow out of. Left unchecked, it is something we will grow deeper into, even as it takes on a more mature appearance over time. We learn to live with it, often by coping with life rather than engaging it for what it actually is. In many ways, it becomes a kind of worldview—one where the world revolves around us.

What the Research Helped Me See

So I began to read and learn. It didn't take long to realize this was not new. For decades, researchers, educators, and parents have been wrestling with the same issue. The language varies, but the core idea is consistent. When children grow up with high levels of comfort and affirmation but relatively little responsibility, entitlement tends to take root, often quietly and unintentionally. When children are consistently protected from hardship and not expected to contribute in meaningful ways, something important is lost. Instead of fostering gratitude, it begins to cultivate expectation. Over time, too much privilege without enough responsibility shapes a posture where more is expected from the world than one is prepared to give in return.

There's an irony in this. As parents, we work hard to create a childhood that is somehow better or more enjoyable than the one we experienced, believing it will lead to greater happiness. And in many ways, it does, for a time. But without responsibility, that comfort can leave our kids unprepared for the realities of adult life, where expectations are higher and the stakes are real.

As Beth Kobliner, author of *Make Your Kid a Money Genius (Before Graduating High School)*, observes,

> Ask parents their greatest wish for their kids, and the answer is usually the same: "We just want them to be happy." Well, sure—that sounds great. But here's the problem: Often the way we try to help our children achieve happiness is by giving them stuff and fun experiences they want. But research tells us that the secret-sauce ingredients to a happy life are hard work, achieving personal goals, and enjoying the satisfaction that comes with the effort.[4]

Kobliner puts words to a quiet tension many parents feel. We want happiness for our children, but we often pursue it in ways that bypass the very experiences that produce it. Effort, responsibility, and meaningful contribution are not obstacles to joy. They are often the pathway to it.

Most parents I talk with are not confused about why entitlement grows. They can see it. They can feel it. The real obstacle is not awareness. It is hesitation, and often a lack of clarity about what to do next. Many parents have already tried to address it. They have set expectations around chores and responsibility, introduced accountability, enforced consequences. And in many cases, the result has been limited, or it has created more tension than traction.

When that is the experience, a deeper fear begins to take hold. We wonder if firmer boundaries will strain the relationship. And when entitlement is already present, and their sense of reality has been shaped by it, simply drawing hard lines often leads to more conflict, not less.

So the fear after failed attempts to enforce responsibility becomes this: What if expecting more and holding the line actually makes things worse? What if it creates more conflict and less connection? That had become my conclusion, and what had led to us softening expectations in our own home. What kept bringing me back to try to enforce things again, however, was the reality that the chores and responsibilities we were asking of our kids were not difficult. In no way were we asking too much of them.

As a result, we drift between extremes. At times we crack down, only to watch our kids buckle under pressure that feels heavy-handed or poorly explained. Then we pull back. We soften. We accommodate. We explain but don't follow through. We extend privileges quickly and quietly lower expectations. In the process, we begin to confuse peace with the absence of conflict.

Again, this approach often produces the very thing we are trying to avoid. Entitlement does not strengthen relationships, it quietly erodes them. When we stepped back and listed out our kids' privileges, we were surprised by how extensive the list had become. Most of it felt normal, just part of everyday life, but they were still privileges – in other words, something they get to enjoy, not something they are owed. Then we looked at real responsibility, not including activities or sports, just what they contributed to the home, and that list was very short in comparison. Somewhere along the way, privilege had really outpaced responsibility, and we were seeing the effects in their attitudes, their effort, and the overall tone of our home.

The Power of Privileges and Responsibility Working Together

After that Thanksgiving table moment in my imagination, I knew I needed clarity. What was actually in our control as parents?

We cannot control outcomes. We cannot control personalities. We cannot control every influence. But we can shape the environment our kids are growing up in. We can set expectations, and establish boundaries and follow-through. And then I had a small moment of clarity. **We can decide whether privilege and responsibility move together or slowly drift apart.**

And if they are going to move together, they need to be connected in a way that is simple and clear. It needs to be something our kids can experience, not just hear about—a cause-and-effect relationship lived out in everyday life, without confusion and without constant lecture.

That realization changed everything. Instead of asking, *How do I get my kids to behave better?* I began asking, *What kind of culture am I building in our home?*

So we made a shift.

We began rethinking how work and responsibility functioned in our home. We built simple structures that carried real weight but required less emotional energy from us as parents. In this system, many privileges were no longer simply given. They were earned and maintained. Technology, being one of the most significant privileges in our home, became the natural place to start. Because privileges had become an expectation, and chores had become optional, we needed to find a remedy that would make privileges special again, and chores meaningful.

So we developed a clear technology plan. Alongside that, we built a chores plan that directly connected responsibility to many privileges, especially technology.

The oversimplified version is that we significantly reduced screen time and put clear boundaries around technology, and we more than doubled chores and responsibilities for each child. On paper, it sounds like a recipe for war! In fact, we were declaring war on entitlement, but this time with an actual plan.

Then we had a formal meeting with the kids and put it into practice.

- We clarified expectations.
- We tied privileges to responsibility.
- We stopped nagging and allowed consistent consequences to do the teaching.

And something unexpected happened.

- The chaos began to settle.
- The tension eased.
- The resentment softened.

Our kids began carrying real responsibility. Not perfectly, but meaningfully. And perhaps most surprising of all, our relationships improved. Part of this agreement, which you'll hear about in later chapters, is that kids are not allowed to escalate emotionally when it's time to do chores or if a chore isn't completed correctly and a privilege is taken away. And, parents agree to not yell, fume, lecture, or nag about chores and consequences. We let the system of privileges and consequences do the work. Therein, the emotional load on parents was greatly diminished.

The Household Economy for Kids

After a week or so, we were hopeful. After a couple of weeks, we were pinching ourselves. After a month, it was clear that this whole thing was working really, really well. The most priceless outcome for me as a dad was that my relationship with my oldest son improved dramatically.

We realized we had created a kind of ecosystem that held things together more clearly in the minds and hearts of our children. It connected everything and gave them a simple way to understand how privileges and responsibility relate. In effect, we had created something our family had been missing: a household economy our kids could understand, and a clear cause-and-effect framework that required far less input from us as parents.

Although *economy* may sound like an overly sophisticated word here, it is actually quite a simple one. It comes from the ancient Greek word *oikonomia*, which literally means "the management of a household." An economy lays out the rules for how people are rewarded (or not rewarded) for working and contributing in a system. In a home, that also includes how privileges are given and maintained. Every home has a kind of household economy, whether it has been named or not. The real question is whether it is clear and livable, or hidden and inconsistent.

In many homes, that system operates in the background. Parents carry the weight and make the decisions, while children simply live within what has been provided. But if they never see the connection between responsibility and privilege, effort and outcome, they remain passive participants.

What we began to build was something more visible. We created a household economy our children could understand—one that was simple, consistent, and lived out in everyday life. In our home, responsibility became the ordinary way many privileges were earned and maintained. No extra pay. No sticker charts. No added rewards. Just a clear reality that helped them understand what they had and what it took to sustain it.

It didn't take long for our kids to begin seeing their role differently, not just as recipients but as contributors. In effect, it created a culture of belonging in the home. The home, in fact, required everyone's help. When the kids heard us routinely say things like 'we need you, we need your help' instead of 'can you help us out?' and then saw how we backed up that reality with a system that was steady, they became willing contributors.

That is why work matters. Work is not just about getting things done; it is one of the primary ways people experience dignity. It forms character and gives shape to privilege. When privilege is disconnected from responsibility, something important is lost.

What surprised us was how little it took to begin changing this dynamic. The privileges did not change. What changed was the connection between privileges and responsibility. As that became clearer, our kids became more grateful, contributed more, and seemed happier for it.

Giving Children What They Need

I didn't write this book because I have everything figured out. But I will say this: The atmosphere in our home today is very different than it was just a few years ago. What surprised me most was not what we learned, but how long it took to arrive at something that proved to be fairly simple.

We found that what our kids ultimately needed was to be more grounded in more reality, which allowed them to become more grateful for what they already had. We didn't need to eliminate their privileges so much as reprioritize ordinary life with chores and responsibility central to their development. Because when kids are grounded in reality and grateful for what they have, they become more reachable.

That's why the intention of this book is to help parents raise grateful and grounded kids in an age of entitlement. Entitlement creep is difficult to recognize because it blends in. Our homes look like the homes around us, which makes it easy to miss what is happening beneath the surface. For us, entitlement was not just a behavior issue. It was shaping how our kids saw the world. And once we saw that, we realized the solution was not about fixing behaviors, but about addressing the system as a whole.

We are standing at a crossroads. We can continue with high privilege and low responsibility and hope it works out. Or we can take ownership of our kids' upbringing by shaping an environment that forms responsibility, work ethic, and perspective over time.

This book is an invitation to give our children what they actually need. Not just to enjoy childhood, but to develop a lasting gratitude that carries into adulthood. Because privilege without responsibility produces entitlement, and entitlement quietly erodes relationships. It may seem harmless in childhood, but it rarely is in adulthood.

We do our children no favors by making life unnecessarily easy. The ease or difficulty they experience in adulthood will be shaped not just by their circumstances, but by their character and their willingness to take ownership and act with initiative.

The Three Areas That Shape the Home

As I worked through this in our own home, it became clear that not every area of life carries equal weight when it comes to forming our kids. There are many influences shaping our children, but a few areas today carry a disproportionate amount of weight. They tend to disrupt the foundation and rhythm of the home, shape daily life, and quietly influence how our kids come to understand the world. For us, three areas consistently rose to the surface:

- Technology
- Work and responsibility in the home
- Money

These are not the only areas that matter. But in today's environment, they are among the most influential. They are influences that when out of balance lead to confusion in our relationships with our kids and leave us grasping for straws.

Technology shapes attention and desire.

Work shapes ownership, contribution, and a sense of belonging.

Money shapes reality around value, tradeoffs, and delayed gratification.

When these three areas begin to align, something powerful happens: **Kids start to understand how life actually works**. They begin to connect effort to outcome, responsibility to privilege, and choices to consequences.

That is what this book is about.

We are going to walk through each of these areas in a practical and livable way, not to create perfect systems but to build a home environment that lays a strong foundation and gives us increased opportunity to have healthy influence in our kids' lives as we prepare them for adulthood. An environment that helps them step into life with clarity, confidence, and a deep sense of responsibility. An environment that helps them become grateful and grounded adults.

Adults who we look forward to sitting across the Thanksgiving table from for years to come.

Financial Literacy Was Still the Goal

Something else became clear as I began working through these areas in our home. They are not independent issues. They are deeply connected.

I originally came into this with a strong focus on financial literacy. That is where most of my experience and conviction lived. I care deeply about helping families prepare their children to understand money, work, and long-term decision-making so they are equipped for adulthood.

But when I tried to have those conversations in my own home, I ran into an unexpected obstacle. The foundation was not there yet. My wife and I realized that entitlement had taken root in subtle ways, not because we were inattentive, but because we had unintentionally allowed privilege to outpace responsibility. And that changed everything. It made meaningful conversations about work, earning, and stewardship difficult, if not impossible. I came to a simple but important realization: I could not teach financial stewardship well in a home that had not first embraced responsibility.

That is what led us to build what we now call a household economy for our kids. Not as a theory, but as a lived system our kids could understand

and participate in. A system that connected privilege to responsibility in a way that was clear, consistent, and sustainable without constant input from us as parents.

Before we walk through how that took shape, it is worth understanding what is at stake and why it matters to lay a strong foundation for responsibility. Today's children are stepping into a financial world that is more complex, less forgiving, and more demanding than the one many of us entered. The realities of habits learned early on around earning, spending, saving, debt, and long-term decision-making carry real consequences. Young adults who leave home without a basic understanding of financial life and how money works are starting at a significant disadvantage.

This is not about raising financial experts. It is about raising financially prepared adults. And if we are going to prepare them well, we need to understand why financial literacy has become essential in the economy they are stepping into.

Big Idea

Modern parenting often gives children high privilege but low responsibility, and that imbalance quietly produces entitlement—something parents must intentionally correct if they want to prepare their kids for adulthood and preserve healthy relationships. Entitlement will erode relationships, especially between parents and kids, during formative years of development. These years are essential for equipping our kids for the future.

Although there are many areas in our kids' lives we are responsible to help shape, three areas carry a disproportionate weight in causing disruption in the home if they are out of balance: technology, chores and responsibility, and money.

When these three issues are connected by a household economy, which knits together effort and outcomes, kids relate to things more easily. Through a system that rewards efforts and responsibility by placing the consequence on privileges they enjoy, we naturally increase the value of privileges and give greater meaning to chores. In so doing, we bring equilibrium and accountability to both.

Chapter 2

Why Financial Literacy Had to Wait

I never intended to write a book on kids and technology, kids and work, *and* kids and finances.

It was always only supposed to be kids and finances.

And truthfully, I never set out to write a book. Over the years, many families asked me questions about raising the financial literacy of their homes. As my own kids got older, I simply began organizing my thoughts and sharing a few short presentations. That's really where this started.

I have long held the conviction that when children grow up understanding how money and finances work, they gain a far more realistic view of adulthood. When kids learn that money is a store of value, that work precedes reward, that saving and investing require patience, that budgeting involves trade-offs, they begin to see life more clearly.

Learning how inflation, loans, taxes, and careers function—and how negotiation, planning, and delayed gratification show up in everyday decisions grounds children in reality. It helps them connect effort to outcome and choice to consequence in ways that abstract instruction alone cannot.

Over time, families who prioritize financial literacy consistently see benefits that extend well beyond dollars and cents. The dividends show up emotionally and relationally as well, shaping children who are more resilient, less reactive, and better prepared to navigate adult responsibilities with perspective and confidence.

In short, children who develop a foundation of financial literacy tend to form healthier relationships, struggle less with impulse as they mature, and carry fewer habits around bad debt into adulthood. These outcomes are not about sophistication or wealth; they are about clarity, self-control, and a growing understanding of how everyday choices compound over time.[5,6,7]

And yet, the broader picture is sobering. According to the 2025 TIAA Institute–GFLEC Personal Finance Index, US adults correctly answered only 49 percent of basic personal finance questions on average—a figure that has remained stubbornly low for years.[8] This points to a persistent gap in financial understanding, even as financial decisions grow more complex and consequential.

I'm familiar with these statistics not just as data, but through years of experience. Although I don't have data to back up this next point, my sense is that financial literacy has been decreasing over the past twenty years among youth and young adults.

To me, financial literacy isn't optional. **It's a manual for how life actually works**. I can't think of a good reason to send my children into adulthood with a high school diploma while leaving them unprepared for the financial decisions that will shape their freedom, stress levels, relationships, and long-term stability for decades to come.

And maybe a 49 percent understanding of basic finances sufficed fifty years ago, or twenty-five years ago, or even ten years ago.

When I think of the changing economic landscape, I can't help but think financial literacy is more important now than it has ever been before.

The Case for Financial Literacy in Childhood

Here are a few reasons I think things have fundamentally changed economically for coming generations. In short, the middle class we've grown up with in America is fundamentally changing; it's getting squeezed, and not in a good way.

Over the past decade or so, the age of first-time homebuyers in the United States has risen steadily. According to data from the National Association of Realtors, the median age of first-time buyers was **about 32 in 2013**, increased to **35 by 2023**, and reached **approximately 38–40 years old by 2024–2025**, the highest level on record.[9]

This shift reflects broader affordability pressures, including rising home prices, higher interest rates, student debt burdens, and delayed household formation, pushing a milestone once common in early adulthood into the late thirties for many Americans.

Where my parents stepped into a booming economy, I benefited from the momentum of that same generational expansion. But that boom has faded into an echo. A different economic landscape has taken shape—one that demands greater discipline, clarity, and intentionality from those coming of age today.

I had a friend purchase a home recently, a fixer-upper in many ways, and his monthly payment (with 10 percent down on the house) is more than $3200/mo. **Just twelve years ago** when we bought our home, our monthly payment was $1200/month for a very similar home in a similar demographic, and with a similar down payment.

Over the past ten to twenty years, **major household costs—especially housing, healthcare, education, and childcare—have risen significantly faster than wages**. While incomes have increased modestly, much of that growth has been absorbed by these essentials, meaning purchasing power for milestones like homeownership or savings has grown far more slowly than headline income numbers suggest.

Let alone saving for retirement; that's a whole other topic.

We have been in an economic boom for eighty years as a nation! As a financial advisor, I'm still super optimistic about the future. However, things have changed fundamentally.

The time to ensure our children leave adolescence with a strong, working understanding of money is **before** they step into adulthood. They need more than abstract knowledge. They need to understand how work actually produces income, how income is limited, and how choices compound over time. They need to see—through lived experience—why saving, investing, and making healthy decisions are not optional skills, but essential tools for navigating real life.

And they need to see it modeled in us as parents.

Adolescence is the window when these lessons can still be practiced safely, when mistakes are instructive rather than catastrophic, and when parents still have meaningful influence. Waiting until full-blown adulthood is often too late. By then, financial decisions come with higher stakes, fewer guardrails, and consequences that linger for years—sometimes decades—often alongside the added weight of student debt.

Helping our kids develop this understanding before they leave our homes is not about turning them into financial experts. It's about giving them clarity—so they can enter adulthood with confidence, restraint, and the ability to make thoughtful decisions in a world where money quietly shapes opportunity, stress, and freedom every single day.

So that's what I set out to do: strengthen financial literacy in our own home and offer that same clarity to other families who wanted it. I genuinely love this work and am grateful for the opportunity to share it with anyone who wants to learn. Money is often misunderstood—not because the principles are complicated or new, but because people lack the confidence to apply what they already know.

In fact, most of the financial-planning clients I work with don't need more information. They already understand the fundamentals: spend less than you earn, save consistently, invest patiently, and avoid unnecessary debt. The challenge is rarely knowledge; it's clarity. When people are faced with several reasonable paths forward, the difficulty isn't determining what could be a good decision. The difficulty is deciding what matters most.

Nearly every option in front of them carries something that feels important: opportunities for their family today, experiences they value, goals they hope to reach someday. Because of that, making one decision often means setting aside another good option, at least for a season. That's where people tend to hesitate. They delay, waiting for perfect clarity that rarely arrives.

What they often need is perspective—in this case, someone to help them step back, weigh what matters most, and move forward with confidence. Because over time, small, wise decisions made early have a powerful compounding effect.

Eventually I began to realize that parenting works much the same way. Most parents aren't confused about what matters. They have good instincts. They can usually sense when something in the home is drifting off course. But when all the competing priorities of family life pile up—school, sports, technology, friendships, busy schedules—it becomes hard to sort out what is most important **right now** versus what will matter most in the **long run**.

A caring parent naturally wants to give their kids good things today: opportunities, experiences, friendships, fun. But at times those good things can compete with the habits and responsibilities that shape a child's future. When everything feels important, it can cloud a parent's judgment and make even simple decisions feel harder than they should.

And again, what's often needed isn't more information. It's clarity, encouragement, and the confidence to decide what matters most today (for the present and in light of the future) and follow through consistently.

And just like investing, the earlier those decisions are made, the more powerful their compounding effect becomes. Small choices made early in a child's life—around responsibility, habits, and expectations—quietly shape the trajectory of the years that follow.

I Had Bigger Fish to Fry First

Well, as it goes, as I began walking out a new plan for developing financial literacy with the kids, I realized I had bigger fish to fry.

As I tried to apply these ideas in our own home, I kept running into the same invisible barrier.

As parents, we began to see a pattern. Before we could talk meaningfully about money, we were already stuck navigating ongoing conflict around chores. Before we could teach delayed gratification, our children's attention was being steadily eroded by technology. And beneath both of those struggles was something harder to name but impossible to ignore: **entitlement**.

Entitlement turned out to be the great disruptor. It quietly distorted how our kids understood effort, privilege, and responsibility. When entitlement was present, money lessons couldn't take root. Saving felt restrictive. Limits felt unfair. Trade-offs felt unnecessary. Not because our children were incapable of understanding, but because the environment around them had already trained a different set of expectations.

To be sure, our home wasn't a land of unlimited screen time and total absence of responsibility either. We had limits and chores in place, they just weren't working in harmony.

What became clear over time was this: **Financial literacy cannot be built on a foundation of entitlement**. Money is downstream from deeper formation.

We eventually realized that before we could develop a healthy sense of financial literacy, we had to wrestle down entitlement itself. That meant addressing the everyday systems that were feeding it—especially the absence of meaningful responsibility with actual accountability and the constant pull of technology. As we clarified expectations, restored contribution in the home, and reclaimed attention, something shifted.

Space opened up.

In fact, sooner than we imagined, there was a renewed sense of harmony in the home. It was, to be honest, something I had assumed was out of reach for us, or something that wasn't to be expected anymore.

And although once we were there it seemed obvious why it was working, getting there felt clunky and confusing.

And once entitlement loosened its grip, financial conversations changed. Money became tangible instead of theoretical. Earning, saving, spending, giving made sense. We even started investing with our teenager. Savings goals became attainable. Trade-offs were learned. Choices carried weight. Delayed gratification started feeling purposeful. Financial literacy was no longer something we were trying to impose; it emerged naturally from the habits already forming.

Today I'm confident my kids will walk away from adolescence with a clear understanding of how powerful money is, why it needs to be a tool and not a treasure, and how to avoid many financial traps young adults find themselves in today.

But, before financial literacy had gridwork, we had to come to grips with privileges, work, responsibility, and technology. This is why this book begins where it does. Not because money is less important, but because **it can only be taught well once entitlement is addressed**. When responsibility, attention, and belonging are restored, financial literacy finally has room to grow—and parents are free to lead with clarity rather than conflict.

Although my initial hope was to focus on kids and finances, it became clear fairly quickly that our family, like many others today, was facing a deeper challenge—one that undermines healthy adolescent development more than money alone: entitlement.

The next chapter does some necessary work in making the case that the culture of our day is shaping our children more powerfully than we often realize—quietly forming their expectations, habits, and assumptions in ways that can work against the development of character, healthy relationships, and a strong work ethic.

We indeed face a major cultural dilemma today in raising our kids to be grateful and grounded adults.

Big Idea

Financial literacy is an essential skill for children entering adulthood, especially in a world where economic decisions are increasingly complex and costly. But financial understanding cannot take root in a home where entitlement is present.

Before children can properly grasp ideas like earning, saving, trade-offs, and delayed gratification, they must first develop a foundation of responsibility and contribution. When privilege exists without meaningful responsibility, money lessons feel restrictive rather than purposeful. Only after parents restore clear expectations around work, attention, and accountability in the home does financial literacy begin to make sense to children.

Chapter 3

How Environment Shapes the Heart

Before we move forward, it's worth pausing for a moment of expectation setting. This chapter is the densest one of the book. Even so, I've been selective in what I include—for two reasons. First, much of what follows is not new or controversial. In many ways, it reflects common sense that has simply become harder to practice in modern life. Second, my goal here is not to sound smarter than I am, but to be as clear and helpful as possible.

This chapter draws from developmental psychology, sociology, economics, theology, and lived experience to explain why certain patterns quietly shape children over time.

The root causes of behavior—especially entitlement—are often difficult to see clearly from the inside. When entitlement takes hold, it distorts a child's sense of reality, making it resistant to logic or explanation. This is not something children can simply be talked out of; it is something they must, over time, *live their way out of.*

When parents understand the forces at work beneath the surface of everyday life, decisions that once felt confusing or exhausting begin to make more sense. The research simply gives language to what many parents already sense but struggle to articulate.

Think of this chapter as laying a foundation. The practical tools and applications that come later are built on this understanding. For some readers, this chapter will be one to move through slowly. For others, it may become a reference you return to over time.

And if you're already on board, feel free to skip ahead to the key takeaways section at the end of the chapter.

The Quiet and Simple Forces Forming Our Children's Hearts

Most parents do not set out to raise entitled children.

We hope to raise kids who are grateful, grounded, capable, and generous. We want them to understand the value of work, to steward money wisely, to build healthy relationships with others, and to move through the world with a sense of responsibility and humility.

What surprises many parents is *how quietly those outcomes are formed.*

Studies across developmental research converge on a single insight: children are shaped far more by daily patterns than by occasional instruction. Formation does not occur primarily through lectures, curriculum, or even well-timed conversations—important as those may be. It happens through lived experience: routines in the home, expectations that are consistently reinforced, and behaviors modeled by parents and other adults.

As author Justin Whitmel Earley observes,

> If our hearts always followed our heads, we would not need to practice the things we learn. We'd just learn about it and the rest would follow. But that's not how humans work, which is why the biblical understanding of sanctification is not just about education and learning but about formation and practice as well.[10]

Children become fluent in the environment in which they are raised. This does not mean they cannot adapt later; it means that their early environment becomes their default. Sort of like a primary language. Learning a second language is always possible, but the farther away from childhood it becomes, the more difficult it is.

Eventually, everyone comes to understand that life is not centered on them. The question is not *if* that realization happens, but *how disruptive it is when it does.*

The modern idea of "adulting" reflects this tension. Tasks that were once assumed as part of growing up now feel surprising or burdensome to many young adults. This reaction is not accidental. It is often the result of childhoods that emphasized comfort and accommodation without sufficient preparation for responsibility.

When children are raised with meaningful responsibility and practical life skills embedded into daily life, adulthood is less disorienting. It is not something to fear, but something they are equipped to enter. Those habits, however, are not absorbed automatically. They are formed by environment—and creating a formative environment requires intentional effort.

Formation Is Already Happening—Whether We Plan It or Not

One of the most helpful shifts parents can make is moving from a mindset of behavior management to one of development. Modern family life is extraordinarily busy, and the pace has changed dramatically in a single generation.

When I was growing up, playing youth hockey meant receiving a printed schedule at the start of the season that changed very little. We did a short tryout, were placed on a team, given a jersey, a picture was taken, there you go. Practices and games were straightforward. Out-of-town tournaments required minimal planning. The season began, the season ended, and life went on.

Today, youth sports come with constant communication and layered expectations. There are weekly email updates, multiple GroupMe (for us) threads per team, and ongoing coordination around logistics, and plenty of volunteer hours. There are pre-season seasons and multiple registrations, and every player gets custom hoodies and hats (which are cool, to be sure). Tournaments are no longer just games—they often include themed events, swag, meals, and experiences designed to make them more memorable.

Much of this is enjoyable, and children certainly have fun. But it also consumes far more time, attention, and energy. As activity volume increases, margins shrink. Quietly, other priorities are displaced because there is simply less space to hold everything at once.

Research consistently shows that while structured activities have value, they are not the primary drivers of developmental growth. Children are shaped most by ordinary, repeated experiences—real responsibility, meaningful contribution, and daily life in the home. These environments may feel less exciting, but over time they are far more influential.

Many children today live with an abundance of activities and a reduced level of responsibility. The result is often overstimulation followed by disengagement. When boredom sets in, many default to screens as a way to check out. Behavioral issues then surface, and because parents are already stretched thin, those issues are often addressed in isolation rather than as part of a larger pattern.

We begin asking tactical questions:

- How do I get my child to listen?
- How do I limit this behavior?
- How do I control this habit?

Important as those questions are, they miss a more formative one: *What story about life is being told by the structure of our home?*

Youth sports like hockey can be meaningful, but for most children they are not preparation for adulthood. When organized activities end, what remains is ordinary life. The real question is whether children have developed the habits and expectations needed to engage that reality with confidence as they move toward adulthood.

Homes quietly teach children what effort looks like, how inconvenience is handled, whether contribution is expected or optional, and whether privilege is treated as a right or a gift. This learning begins long before children can articulate values or understand intent.

In modern households, three forces do an outsized amount of this formative work:

1. Technology
2. Work within the home
3. Money

And we are going to introduce the influence of these three topics in that order.

Each of these shapes children's habits, expectations, and understanding of how life works. Whether they are present, absent, or poorly structured has a lasting effect. The patterns children internalize during childhood strongly influence their confidence, resilience, and sense of purpose as they move toward independent adulthood.

Technology, in particular, exerts a powerful formative influence. Beyond concerns about inappropriate content or online harm, its deeper impact is behavioral. When children are not guided in how to regulate their time and use, technology trains distraction—undermining attention, patience, and the ability to engage meaningfully with ordinary responsibilities.

Technology: Attention Is a Moral Environment

Technology does not merely occupy time. It trains attention.

Attention shapes what children notice, what they ignore, what they pursue, and what they avoid. Over time, it forms patience, self-regulation, empathy, and the capacity to remain present in moments that are slow, difficult, or unstimulating.

In *The Opt-Out Family: How to Give Your Kids What Technology Can't*, Erin Loechner examines the long-term effects of technology, social media, and constant screen exposure as children grow toward adulthood. Drawing from her experience working within the social media industry, she asks a sobering question about the future: "Who will be left behind?" Her answer is both simple and unsettling: "The child who cannot concentrate."[11]

Andy and Amy Crouch, writing to young people in *My Tech-Wise Life*, describe this dynamic with this great point: "But our devices don't encourage one-time, moderate distractions. Rather, they encourage a posture of distraction."[12]

This posture matters because distraction does more than interfere with productivity. **It blinds children to what is happening in their own hearts.** One teenage participant in an example referencing ten minutes of quiet reflection time at a youth retreat in Crouch's work described the fear that surfaced when distraction was removed: "I don't want to be alone with my thoughts—they're too painful."[13]

That admission reveals something profound. When children are never asked to sit with boredom, frustration, or silence, they lose opportunities to develop emotional resilience and self-awareness. Screens become not just entertainment, but avoidance.

This is why the research consistently shows that the problem is not simply *how much* screen time children have, but **what screens replace**. What many children are losing is unstructured time, unscheduled boredom, and repeated opportunities to work through discomfort—conditions that are essential for developing resilience, patience, and maturity.

In other words, boredom is not a problem to solve but a gift to protect. The next time you hear, "Mom, Dad, I'm bored," take heart. Something formative may be happening beneath the surface!

Technology Is Often Anti-Boredom

As Crouch notes, children under fourteen now spend nearly twice as much time with technology as they do in conversation with their families. That imbalance quietly reshapes expectations. Effort feels unreasonable. Waiting feels unnecessary. Boredom becomes intolerable.

One of the great ironies of modern parenting is our fear of boredom.

Yet research across education and developmental psychology consistently shows that boredom is not harmful; it is a gateway state. It creates the pause necessary for creativity, initiative, and self-direction to emerge. Crouch captures this simply: "'The cure for boredom is not distraction. It's wonder.' The poet Gerard Manley Hopkins wrote, 'The world is charged with the grandeur of God.'"[14]

When children are not immediately rescued from boredom, they begin to discover capacities they did not know they had. They learn to initiate play, tolerate frustration, and engage meaningfully with their surroundings. In these spaces, work stops feeling like punishment and starts to feel like participation.

Technology does not merely occupy time; it trains attention. Attention shapes what children notice, what they ignore, what they pursue, and what they avoid. Over time, it shapes capacities like patience, self-regulation, empathy, and the ability to remain present in moments that are slow, difficult, or unentertaining.

That posture matters because distraction does more than reduce productivity; it dulls self-awareness.

The Myth of Neutral Technology

Modern parents are often told that technology is inevitable, and that the goal is simply to teach children to "use it responsibly." But as Loechner notes, this framing misunderstands the asymmetry at play: "According to Tristan Harris . . . the problem isn't that people lack willpower, it's that there are a thousand people on the other side of the screen whose job it is to break down the self-regulation you have."[15]

Algorithms are not designed to cultivate wisdom, patience, or contentment. They are engineered to maximize engagement, often by leveraging fear, anger, comparison, and desire. Major technology companies invest extraordinary resources in designing systems that keep users—especially children—from disengaging.

The incentive structure is straightforward. Attention drives advertising. Advertising drives revenue. Every moment a user disengages represents lost profit. In this environment, families are not competing on equal footing. Parents are asking children to delay, limit, or abstain, while companies deploy elite engineering talent and massive capital to capture and hold attention.

We are living in a "Wild West" phase of technological advancement—rapid growth, minimal guardrails, and incentives heavily tilted toward expansion. There is too much market share at stake and too much revenue on the line for companies to meaningfully slow engagement on their own. As a result, parental concerns about limits, controls, and boundaries are often acknowledged rhetorically but rarely addressed structurally.

This is why limits are not punitive; they are formative. As Justin Whitmel Earley observes through a theological lens: "In the American story, limits are bad. They get in the way of our freedom. But in the story of God, limits are the way to the good life—even the way to happiness."[16]

Children raised in environments with clear, consistent limits around technology are not being deprived. They are being trained in discernment. Attention requires boundaries.

The technological landscape children are navigating today is fundamentally different from the one many parents grew up with. This is no longer a matter of simple entertainment. Today's digital environments are complex, adaptive systems designed to capture and hold attention. Treating them casually underestimates their formative power.

Because of all its potential, technology is also an incredible privilege.

Privilege and Gratitude

One of the most common things parents say is, "I just want my kids to be more grateful."

But gratitude is not something that can be lectured into existence.

Gratitude is often emphasized in churches—and rightly so. Those of us who have experienced grace have much to be thankful for. My own life was radically redirected in early adulthood, and I am deeply aware that my present circumstances are a gift. That awareness, however, did not come primarily from instruction. It came from lived experience. It came from perspective.

Entitlement is often rooted in a lack of perspective. While perspective can be borrowed briefly through hearing another person's story, it is most deeply formed through one's own experience. Many people do not fully recognize what they have until hardship or loss exposes it. These moments are painful, but they often become the soil in which gratitude and a clearer understanding of grace grow.

Children develop perspective in the same way—through experience.

When children have no meaningful ability to lose privileges, those privileges are rarely experienced as gifts. They become expectations. By contrast, when privileges are earned, maintained, and connected to contribution and ownership, children experience the dignity of effort and the satisfaction of overcoming challenges.

Psychological research consistently supports this pattern: gratitude grows when benefits are perceived as both valuable and costly. When provision is automatic, invisible, or disconnected from effort, gratitude struggles to take root. Homes that remove friction from everything—instant entertainment, instant purchases, instant solutions—often do so with good intentions, yet unintentionally cultivate entitlement.

Privileges are powerful, and they are rarely neutral. Over time, they shape either gratitude or entitlement, depending on whether or not they are paired with perspective, responsibility, and contribution.

Ordinary Life Is More Important Than We Realize

As I mentioned earlier, one of the motivations behind this book is how obvious these principles are—and yet how difficult they have become to sustain in daily home life over time. The challenge is not confusion; it is consistency.

In practical terms, it is often easier to fill children's schedules with activities, sports, and entertainment than it is to engage them in ongoing household responsibility. That imbalance is not accidental. It reflects the extraordinary level of abundance we now live with. The fact that many families do not *need* their children's help at home says a great deal about modern privilege.

What we are confronting, then, is not a complex problem but a subtle one. Gradual cultural shifts toward comfort and convenience dull our sense of what is necessary. Over time, common-sense practices are displaced, and we forget that ordinary, shared responsibility is a primary way children grow into capable adults who experience genuine gratitude.

Healthy formation does not demand perfect parenting or heroic interventions. It requires **attention to the ordinary**.

When technology and privilege outpace responsibility, entitlement often follows. Children begin to feel little need to contribute at home, and earning money can seem unnecessary when most needs and wants are already met. Over time, comfort dulls the urgency to grow, quietly weakening preparation for adulthood—often in ways that don't become visible until years later.

There are few things in life uglier than a child who demands their privileges as though they were needs. From personal experience, I can also say there are few things more precious than when a once-spoiled or entitled child begins to recognize what they truly have and their heart shifts toward gratitude. It's a bit like Ebenezer Scrooge on Christmas morning: when he finally sees clearly what matters and embraces a new way of living, and those around him embrace him in return. But in his story, as in real life, that kind of change usually begins with a wake-up call.

Work in the Home: Why Participation Shapes the Heart

If technology shapes attention and money shapes desire, **work in the home shapes belonging.**

Few areas of parenting are as misunderstood—or as powerfully formative—as children participating in the everyday work of the household. In many modern families, chores are treated as an inconvenience, a bargaining chip, or a disciplinary tool. But research consistently shows that meaningful work in the home is one of the most reliable ways to cultivate competence, self-regulation, and long-term well-being.

The question is not whether children should help at home, rather how can the child begin to believe their help is needed in the home and become engaged in a meaningful way.

The University of Minnesota Findings: Early Work, Lasting Outcomes

A number of contemporary parenting and formation authors point to long-running longitudinal research conducted at the University of Minnesota, often associated with researcher Marty Rossmann, when discussing the long-term impact of childhood responsibility. This research followed children into early adulthood and identified that one of the strongest predictors of later success was not IQ, not extracurricular involvement, not family income, but early participation in household work.

Children who began helping with age-appropriate tasks as early as ages three or four were consistently described as demonstrating

- greater academic competence
- stronger social skills

- higher levels of self-confidence
- better early-career outcomes in their twenties

The conclusion was not that chores mechanically produce achievement, but that early contribution fosters a sense of capability and belonging that carries forward into adulthood. Children who grow up seeing themselves as contributors internalize a different narrative about life: *I am needed. I can help. I have something to offer.*

As I've shared during my workshops on this topic, "Work provides our children opportunities to feel included in the family in ways nothing else can." Work is not merely practical help. It is identity formation.

Justin Whitmel Earley echoes this in theological language: "The household is a little school of love, a place where our vocation is to form all who live there into lovers of God and neighbor."[17] And much of this happens by helping them discover their gifts, their personalities, their unique makeup in relationship to serving God and serving others, beginning with the family.

Children do not learn that they belong by being entertained. They learn that they belong by being needed! When kids are invited into the work of the home—not because they are efficient, but because they are family—they begin to internalize a powerful truth: *My presence matters here.*

Why Efficiency Is the Wrong Metric

One of the reasons parents quietly abandon chores is efficiency. It is faster to do the work ourselves. It is cleaner. It is easier. And we avoid emotional struggles with children who make us feel insane when we repeat ourselves over, and over, and . . . over.

But efficiency is a poor goal for development. Earley says it this way: "If the main goal of work was efficiency, we would never invite kids into work. Their help is almost guaranteed to hurt. But what if the goal of work is not to get it done as fast as possible? What if work is far more spiritual than that?"[18]

Work done together—slowly, messily, and relationally—forms patience, humility, and perseverance. These are not taught in lectures. They are practiced.

When children receive the benefits of family life without participating in its upkeep, something subtle but important happens: **they begin to believe that nothing is required of them as a member of the family.** As such, the privileges they have are theirs to keep, and anything that threatens to take them away is antagonistic to the child.

As such, privileges either lead to gratitude or entitlement.

Why Parents Get Stuck: Fear, Fatigue, and Frustration

Many parents know chores matter. So why do so many struggle to follow through?

Some of the top reasons, for me and many others, are as follows:

- Lack of time
- Lack of clarity
- Parental frustration
- Inconsistent accountability
- Fear of damaging the relationship

These are realities of modern family life. But research suggests that avoiding these tensions does not preserve relationship. It quietly erodes it.

Homes without shared contribution often experience

- increased resentment from parents
- increased entitlement from children
- more frequent conflict, not less

Many parents—myself included—are doing their best with the time, energy, and clarity they have, yet still feel frustrated or disappointed by how their kids respond to responsibility. That frustration is understandable.

But this matters: When our approach to chores and expectations is driven primarily by irritation or disappointment, our influence with our children begins to fade. The issue is rarely a lack of care or effort on the parent's part. More often, it is a lack of clarity.

The solution is not harsher enforcement. It is clearer structure.

Structure as a Gift, Not a Threat

Children do not experience structure as oppressive when it is consistent, predictable, and fair. They experience it as safety.

A household chore plan functions in much the same way. It does not create maturity or responsibility on its own, but it provides the structure that allows healthy development to take place over time.

Children flourish when they know

- what is expected
- when it is expected

- what happens if it is not done
- that parents will respond calmly and consistently

Structure frees parents from nagging and frees children from constant negotiation.

Money, Childhood, and the Formation of a Money Script

Chores and thoughtful technology boundaries have become essential guides in the modern home. When it comes to the formation of our children, they lay a strong foundation, creating the structure upon which other important lessons can be built.

One of the areas where I am most convinced children gain a lasting advantage—both in life and in contentment—is in how they learn to handle money. Yet the way children absorb financial understanding is often different from how we assume.

One of the most important truths about money is that our relationship with it begins forming long before we are aware of it. In childhood, money is not primarily taught; it is caught. Through what children see, what they have access to, and how parents talk about money—or avoid talking about it—they begin forming what researchers often call a *money script*: a set of deeply ingrained assumptions about how money works and what it means.

A money script functions much like an operating system. It runs quietly in the background, shaping decisions, reactions, fears, and habits without drawing attention to itself. Over time, it influences how we spend, save, give, take risks, avoid risks, and measure success. And like most operating systems, it is difficult to identify and even harder to rewrite later in life. By adulthood, many people are living out financial patterns they never consciously chose—and often struggle to explain.

This is why childhood matters so much. The habits and examples children experience early on do more than shape behavior; they shape identity. When money is invisible, touchless, and constantly available, children may internalize the belief that provision is automatic and limits are unnecessary. When money is connected to effort, choices, and trade-offs, children begin to understand that money is a tool—not a source of identity or worth. In an age of technology, this formation is under constant pressure.

Comparison is no longer occasional; it is relentless. Social media, advertising, and algorithm-driven content place curated versions of other people's lives directly in front of our children every day. Without intentional formation, it becomes easy for kids to equate happiness with having more, being more, or keeping up. In that environment, helping children develop healthy money habits is no longer optional; it is essential to cultivating self-control, perspective, and a clear sense of what actually matters.

If we want our children to grow into adults who work hard, take ownership of their lives, and learn to be content with what they have—rather than trapped in the exhausting cycle of always wanting more—we must give them a healthier money script than the culture offers. That script is written through repeated, embodied experiences in childhood: earning, allocating, waiting, choosing, giving, and sometimes doing without. Over time, these practices quietly teach children that money is a servant, not a master—and that a good life is built on stewardship, not accumulation.

One of the most valuable habits children can develop—and one that research consistently links to greater satisfaction in both careers and relationships—is the ability to delay gratification. Money provides an especially practical way for children to practice this skill without needing lengthy explanations or abstract lessons.

Once again, for children, more is caught than taught. As they learn to save, wait, plan, and make trade-offs, they are not just managing money; they are forming habits that shape patience, self-control, and perspective. In the process, they begin building a healthy internal operating system for life, often without realizing it and without us needing to spell it out.

Work, Money, Financial Literacy, and the Formation of Delayed Gratification

Household work becomes even more formative when it is paired thoughtfully with money. Money, handled well, becomes a laboratory for delayed gratification—one of the strongest predictors of long-term stability, satisfaction, and emotional maturity. It helps children understand a basic reality of adult life: Effort precedes income, income is limited, and every decision involves trade-offs.

Financial literacy at this stage is not about sophistication. It is about clarity. The goal is not to raise children who are "good with money," but children who understand limits, choices, and consequences. That understanding is built through experience, not instruction.

When children earn money—through household work, outside jobs, or age-appropriate opportunities—they begin to grasp that income is connected to contribution. Money stops feeling abstract. It becomes finite. Spending one dollar means not spending it somewhere else. Saving requires saying no in the present for the sake of something later. These are not lessons that can be absorbed through explanation alone; they must be lived.

This is why allocation matters. Giving children simple categories—spending, saving, giving—forces visible choices. Saving gains meaning when it is attached to a purpose rather than treated as accumulation. Spending becomes instructional when children live with the outcome of a poor decision. Giving reminds them that money is not only personal, but relational.

As children mature, they also benefit from exposure to the real constraints of adult finances, like understanding that gross pay is not the same as take-home pay. Learning that prices rise over time also helps them see why planning matters and why money left idle loses power. Seeing how debt pulls future resources into the present teaches restraint far more effectively than warnings ever could.

Repeatedly choosing to wait, to plan, and to live within limits trains patience and self-control—traits that research consistently links to long-term satisfaction. As Morgan Housel observes, "Financial success is not a hard science. It's a soft skill, where how you behave is more important than what you know."[19]

When money is introduced this way, it does more than teach math or mechanics. It teaches children how the world actually works. It prepares them to temper impulse, understand trade-offs, and avoid the trap of believing that more automatically leads to better. In doing so, it helps protect them from entitlement and equips them with habits that extend far beyond finances.

When work and money are paired intentionally in the home, children are not being rushed into adulthood. They are being given the tools to enter it with perspective, restraint, and confidence.

Why Work Must Not Always Be Paid

Something else that I found interesting in my research is the topic of allowances. It is a strangely polarizing topic. Some believe it is the first step to creating a welfare state in the mind of a child, while others think it's a great way for kids to learn to handle money before earning money is realistic or age appropriate.

The reality is this: Research does not show that allowances in and of themselves help or hinder a child's personal development toward gratitude and responsibility.

Research does, however, show that having kids do chores and work in the home that are NOT paid for creates a psychological bond to the family and a sense of belonging to the home that is incredibly beneficial for their development.

As such, these experts share that ideally allowances may be better suited to be just "given" as a means of giving your kids some money to learn to handle, and less about a reward for completing chores. This allowance can be the money they have choice over when it comes to your trips to Target, or to an event where there is a concession stand; instead of offering to buy them something, you can invite them to consider how they want to use their allowance money.

Completing chores as part of the family has greater emotional benefit to the child when a reward is not present. And when every task is monetized, children may internalize the belief that contribution is transactional rather than relational.

We will return to the topic of allowances and jobs that earn money later.

Bringing It All Together

Technology shapes attention.

Work shapes belonging.

Money shapes desire.

Together, they form an ecosystem of formation.

When screens dominate, when work disappears, and when money feels frictionless, children are trained—quietly—to expect comfort without contribution.

When we increase privilege without increasing responsibility, we increase the odds of entitlement ruling over our children. **And entitlement erodes the relationship so many of us long to have with our kids that exist beyond the years they are under our roof.**

When privileges are attached to responsibility, when work is shared, and when money is handled intentionally, children are invited into a different story:

- Life includes effort.
- Belonging includes participation.
- Provision is a gift, not a guarantee.

This is not about control. It is about stewardship. And stewardship, like formation, begins at home.

So here's the oversimplified plan this book reaches toward:

1. Limit technology's reach.
2. Increase responsibility.
3. Teach financial literacy.

When privilege is structured well, it leads to gratitude rather than entitlement.

A Pastoral Word to Parents

How are you feeling after reading all of this? Most parents are not failing; they are tired. We are raising children in a cultural moment that pulls relentlessly toward speed, convenience, entertainment, and comparison. Against that backdrop, intentional homes will always feel slightly countercultural.

The research, however, is encouraging. Small, consistent changes reshape family culture faster than most parents expect. Children are remarkably adaptable. They rise to expectations when those expectations are clear, fair, and sustained.

---

20 Key Takeaways

1. **Formation happens quietly and continuously**. Children are shaped far more by daily patterns and lived experience than by occasional instruction, lectures, or conversations.
2. **Environment matters more than intention**. Good intentions alone do not prevent entitlement or cultivate gratitude; the structure of the home does the real formative work.
3. **Children become fluent in the environment they grow up in**. Early childhood experiences function like a primary language. Later change is possible, but harder.
4. **Modern childhood emphasizes comfort over preparation**. Many children experience high levels of accommodation, activity, and entertainment with comparatively little responsibility, making adulthood more disorienting.
5. **Three forces do much of the formative work in modern homes**:
    - **Technology** shapes attention.
    - **Work in the home** shapes belonging.
    - **Money** shapes desire.

6. **Technology trains attention, not just behavior.** Screens do not merely consume time; they condition distraction, impatience, and avoidance of discomfort.
7. **Boredom is not harmful; it is formative.** Unstructured time creates the conditions for creativity, resilience, initiative, and emotional regulation.
8. **Limits are not punitive; they are formative.** Clear, consistent boundaries help children know the boundaries and develop patience and self-control.
9. **Gratitude cannot be taught through instruction alone.** Gratitude grows through perspective, effort, and lived experience—especially the ability to lose or delay privileges.
10. **Privilege is never neutral.** When privilege is disconnected from responsibility, entitlement grows quietly and predictably.
11. **Work in the home forms belonging.** Children learn they matter not by being entertained, but by being needed.
12. **Efficiency is the wrong metric for formation.** Work done slowly, imperfectly, and together forms character, patience, and perseverance.
13. **Structure functions as a gift, not a threat.** Predictable expectations provide safety and reduce conflict for both parents and children.
14. **Money formation begins in childhood through experience.** Children develop "money scripts" based on what they observe, practice, and experience—not what they are told.
15. **Financial literacy is about clarity, not sophistication.** Understanding limits, trade-offs, and consequences comes through lived financial experience.
16. **Delayed gratification is one of the most valuable life skills children can learn.** Work and money together provide a natural laboratory for practicing patience, restraint, and planning.
17. **Not all work should be paid.** Unpaid household responsibility fosters belonging and relational contribution, not transaction. When everything is monetized, contribution will often feel transactional.
18. **Formation is an ecosystem.** Technology, work, and money interact to shape attention, belonging, and desire. Together they cultivate grounded living and the basis for perspective and gratitude.
19. **High privilege paired with low responsibility produces entitlement.** Boundaries, shared work, and intentional money practices

invite children into a different story—one of stewardship rather than consumption.

20. **Entitlement erodes relationship**. If what we want with our kids is lasting relationship, we must guard against entitlement. Entitlement breeds resistance to responsibility and resentment toward anything that threatens privilege. Gratitude, by contrast, forms the foundation for humility and a life open to giving and receiving.

Chapter 4

The Role of Responsibility and Grace

The question before parents is no longer whether childhood has changed, because we know it has based on the research we just explored. Now we need to explore what actually shapes the opposite of entitlement.

Scripture, experience, and centuries of wisdom point to a clear answer: responsibility. Not responsibility as punishment. Not responsibility as pressure. But responsibility as the primary way gratitude, humility, resilience, and maturity take root in a person's life.

This chapter moves beneath behavior and beneath systems. It is not about tactics or tools. It is about what daily life is quietly teaching the heart over time—why responsibility is one of the most loving gifts we can give both children and disciples.

Growth Happens Through Practice, Not Intention

One of the most common misunderstandings in parenting and discipleship is the belief that good intentions naturally lead to good outcomes. We assume that if we love our children well, explain things clearly, and model decent behavior, the deeper virtues will eventually emerge on their own.

But people are not shaped primarily by what they *intend.*

They are shaped by what they *practice.*

Growth happens through repetition—through lived experience and the slow accumulation of habits that train how a person sees the world and understands their place within it. Over time, practice forms instinct. It shapes default responses long before conscious reflection catches up.

This concern sits at the heart of theologian Dallas Willard's critique of what he called *non-discipleship*. Willard observed that many Christians sincerely believe the right things yet do not become people who actually live differently. The problem, he argued, was not a lack of belief, but a lack of embodied practice—a life intentionally trained around following Jesus.

In *The Spirit of the Disciplines*, he writes,

> The greatest issue facing the world today, with all its heartbreaking needs, is whether those who are identified as "Christians" will become disciples—students, apprentices, practitioners—of Jesus Christ, steadily learning from him how to live the life of the Kingdom of the Heavens into every corner of human existence.[20]

Children develop in the same way. They do not become grateful because we talk about gratitude. They become grateful because they have lived within limits, contributed to others, and received good things in the context of effort. Responsibility is the practice that teaches that way of seeing.

Grace Is Not Opposed to Effort

We worry that asking too much might hurt the relationship or discourage our kids. This is where one of Willard's most quoted lines matters deeply: "Grace is not opposed to effort; it is opposed to earning."[21] Effort is not the enemy of grace. It is the way grace does its work. Grace does not remove responsibility; it gives it meaning.

When life becomes centered on earning—proving worth, securing approval, or avoiding failure—something very different begins to grow. Work and effort become anxious and transactional. Success breeds pride, failure breeds shame, and relationships begin to revolve around performance rather than love.

Grace interrupts that pattern. It allows effort to remain meaningful without making a person's value depend on the outcome. When parents remove responsibility in the name of grace, children are often left with comfort but without the inner strength needed to carry life when comfort is absent. Responsibility, held within love, is how grace becomes tangible in everyday life.

Entitlement Is Something Children Learn

Entitlement is not something children wake up and choose. It develops when desire is repeatedly fulfilled without effort, limits, or contribution.

Ron Lieber, in *The Opposite of Spoiled*, describes entitlement not as having too much, but as expecting too much. Children are not defined by what they possess, but by what they assume should be provided. Lieber writes, "Spoiling is not about what children have. It's about what they expect—and what they don't understand about how the world works."[22]

That sentence is worth sitting with. Entitlement is a way of interpreting reality. It trains children to see the world as something that should accommodate them rather than something they are meant to participate in. Responsibility reshapes that interpretation.

Responsibility Changes Relationships

One of the most damaging effects of entitlement is relational. When responsibility is absent, relationships quietly reorganize themselves around self-service rather than mutual care. Parents drift into the role of provider and fixer. Children drift into the role of consumer. Gratitude fades. Resentment grows quietly on both sides.

Avoiding responsibility does not preserve innocence. It creates a vacuum. And vacuums are always filled—by peers, screens, comparison, and desire without limits. Responsibility protects relationships because it teaches children how to live *with* others, not just alongside them.

Responsibility Steadies Children

Many parents fear that responsibility will overwhelm their children. In practice, the opposite is often true. Children are calmer when expectations are clear. They are less anxious when boundaries are predictable. Responsibility provides structure in a world that often feels chaotic.

Scripture affirms this repeatedly. Proverbs connects wisdom with discipline not because discipline is harsh, but because it is protective. Hebrews describes discipline as evidence of belonging, not rejection.

Responsibility answers questions children are always asking, even when they cannot put them into words:

What is expected of me?

Where do I fit?

Can I trust the adults around me to lead?

When responsibility is absent, children test limits to find those answers. When it is present, children can rest.

Responsibility Is How Independence Grows

Maria Montessori's insight is often summarized poetically, but her point was practical and developmental.

Montessori observed that independence does not appear because adults decide a child is ready. It grows out of responsibility. In her early classrooms, children were not given freedom apart from structure; they were given freedom through meaningful work. When children were responsible for caring for their work and classroom environment—cleaning, restoring order, handling materials with care—they became calmer, more focused, and more capable.

Maria observed, over thousands of hours of scientific observation of children, that when children in a classroom were responsible for the care of their own workspaces AND the entire classroom, they were better behaved, were more engaged in work, had greater respect for their peers, and greater respect for their teacher.[23]

Responsibility did not restrict freedom. Rather, it created it. This mirrors the Christian vision of discipleship. Jesus offers apprenticeship: "Take My yoke upon you and learn from Me, for I am gentle and lowly in heart, and you will find rest for your souls. For My yoke is easy and My burden is light" (Matthew 11:29–30).

Learning requires effort, repetition, and submission. And paradoxically, that yoke becomes the place of rest. Responsibility teaches children—and disciples of all ages—how to use freedom wisely rather than waste it.

Parenting and Discipleship Follow the Same Pattern

What is true for children is true for disciples of all ages. Faith is practiced. Gratitude is cultivated. Responsibility is carried. Discipleship that avoids effort produces shallow faith. Parenting that avoids responsibility produces fragile children. Growth always involves participation.

Homes structured around responsibility, limits, and grace quietly disciple long before children can articulate theology. They learn that life is not about consumption, but stewardship. That freedom is not detached from responsibility. That joy grows where gratitude takes root.

Childhood is the season in which we quietly build the trellis that allows children to grow into grateful and grounded adults. Without a trellis, growth sprawls and fruit never reaches the light. Without good soil, seeds struggle to take root. And without grace, gratitude is reduced to behavior rather than becoming a way of life.

A Pastoral Word to Parents

As I began rethinking how responsibility and structure function in our own home, my concern was not whether change was needed; it was how to pursue it wisely. I was aware that my children could already experience me as heavy-handed at times, and the last thing I wanted was to reinforce that dynamic in the name of doing what was "right."

What I lacked in that season was not conviction, but clarity.

Like most parents, my wife and I wanted good things for our children, including good behavior. But behavior, I've learned, is a poor primary goal. It is a signal, not the destination. When behavior becomes the focus, we often miss the deeper work of formation that shapes who our children are becoming.

The aim of this framework is not control, compliance, or short-term order. It is to ground our children in a life worth living—one that is realistic, resilient, and capable of carrying adulthood without unnecessary drama. My hope is that we foster a childhood our children might one day look back on and say, "That's the kind of home I want to build."

For parents who tend toward intensity or firmness—I include myself here—this distinction matters. Much of what follows is intentionally designed to shift the weight off personality and onto shared structures. When expectations are clear and systems are consistent, emotion and reactivity no longer have to do the heavy lifting.

Structure, held with grace, protects both relationship and joy.

Why This Chapter Comes Before the How-To

Without this foundation, everything that follows can feel distorted.

Chores feel harsh.

Privileges feel controlling.

Work feels transactional.

With this foundation, those same practices feel humane and wise.

Responsibility feels loving.

Structure feels protective.

Effort feels dignifying.

Responsibility does not destroy joy. It helps it grow.

Big Idea

Responsibility is the primary pathway through which gratitude, maturity, and resilience are formed by consistent practice embedded in daily life. When children live within clear limits, contribute meaningfully, and experience effort within the context of grace, they develop a grounded understanding of their place in the world.

Entitlement, by contrast, grows when privilege is detached from responsibility. Far from harming relationships, responsibility strengthens them by fostering mutual care and consideration. It also provides stability, clarity, and a foundation for true independence. Ultimately, responsibility—held together with grace—is one of the most loving gifts parents can give their children.

Chapter 5

Childhood Is Practice for Adulthood

One of the most important shifts parents can make is learning to see childhood not as a performance to manage or a season to survive, but as preparation for adulthood.

That may sound obvious, but many of the pressures parents feel today come from quietly holding a different assumption. We treat childhood as something to protect from difficulty, to fill with opportunity, or to curate carefully so our kids don't fall behind. In doing so, we can lose sight of what childhood is actually for.

Your children's childhood is not meant to be a future country-hit single about looking back to the "good old days" when life was fun and easy. Don't be Uncle Rico.

Childhood is practice.

It is the long, slow (but enjoyable!) rehearsal for adult life—how to live with others, how to handle responsibility, how to respond when things don't go your way, how to work, how to wait, how to give, and how to take ownership of your life.

When we forget that, we unintentionally prepare kids for comfort instead of competence.

The Gap Between Childhood and Adulthood

One reason parenting feels harder today is that the gap between childhood expectations and adult expectations has grown wider.

In adulthood, no one reminds you repeatedly to show up on time. No one negotiates whether you feel like doing your job. Bills don't wait until you're in the right mood. Relationships require patience, compromise, and effort even when you're tired. Technology is not regulated for you. Money runs out if you don't manage it.

But many modern childhoods look very different. Schedules are built around kids' activities. Adults intervene quickly when things are uncomfortable. Consequences are delayed or softened. Responsibility is often optional. Discomfort is treated as something to solve rather than something to learn from.

Then adulthood arrives, and it feels harsh. What's changed is not adulthood. **What's changed is childhood.**

When kids grow up practicing adulthood in small, age-appropriate ways, adulthood feels familiar. When they don't, it feels overwhelming and unfair.

Why Structure Is Loving

Structure often gets a bad reputation. It can sound cold, rigid, or controlling. But healthy structure does the opposite of what many parents fear—it creates safety.

Children are calmer when expectations are clear. They are less anxious when boundaries are predictable. And they feel more secure when adults lead with confidence rather than uncertainty.

Structure quietly answers questions children are always asking, even when they cannot articulate them:

- What is expected of me?
- What happens if I don't follow through?
- Can I trust the adults in my life to hold things together?

When structure is absent or inconsistent, children respond by testing limits. This testing is not rebellion; it is information seeking. Children are trying to discover where the lines are and whether anyone is truly in charge.

Both Maria Montessori and Lev Vygotsky help clarify this dynamic. Montessori observed that children push against unclear limits not to defy authority, but to understand how the world works. Vygotsky described this same space as the *Zone of Proximal Development*—the place where a child stretches just beyond what they already know, learning through guidance, feedback, and practice.

Put simply, children test boundaries because boundaries teach. Limits show them what is possible, what is safe, and what is expected. When limits are missing, children keep pushing because the learning task is unfinished.

Clear, consistent structure does not restrict development; it supports it. Boundaries create the conditions in which self-control can grow and wisdom can eventually be internalized. Structure removes the burden of uncertainty so children can focus on learning and growth.

The same principle applies to creativity. Boundaries and constraints do not stifle creativity; they give it shape. Creativity has meaning because of limits: time, resources, relationships, responsibility. God consistently invites us to steward what we *have*, not wish for what we do not.

This is why healthy discipline, at its best, is not punishment; it is guidance. It is the steady presence of an adult who says, "This is how life works, and I'm here to help you learn."

Why Parents Fear Structure

Many parents hesitate to create structure because they are afraid it will damage the relationship. And, it doesn't usually come very naturally.

Structure takes time to develop. It requires consistency and accountability. And it has to adapt as children grow.

Underneath that hesitation are deeper fears:

- Parents don't want to be the bad guy.
- They don't want constant conflict.
- They don't want their children to feel controlled or unloved.

Those fears are understandable—especially in a culture that often equates love with affirmation and freedom. But structure and relationship are not opposites. In many cases, structure actually protects the relationship over time.

When expectations are unclear, parents end up nagging. When consequences are inconsistent, parents end up negotiating. When boundaries are flexible, parents become exhausted—repeating themselves, raising their voices, and slipping into long lectures. If nagging were an effective parenting strategy, most of us would be finished by now. It isn't.

Nagging wears children down, and over time it wears down the relationship as well. Clear structure reduces friction. It allows parents to stop arguing about everything and start leading calmly. And children often feel more respected—not less—when adults are confident enough to lead.

At the same time, structure can go too far. Homes that become overly rigid or controlling can stifle the very curiosity and independence we hope our children will develop. The goal is not control. The goal is guidance—structure strong enough to create stability, but flexible enough to allow children to grow.

Discipline as Investment, Not Control

Discipline is one of the most misunderstood words in parenting. Many people hear it and think of punishment or control. But discipline, at its core, means training—for growth, for practice, for mistakes.

Athletes aren't trained by being yelled at every time they fail. They're trained through repetition, correction, encouragement, and clear expectations. Parenting works the same way. Discipline says, "This matters enough to practice."

When parents discipline with that mindset, kids experience it differently. They may not like it in the moment, but they understand—often later—that someone cared enough to help them grow.

Letting Kids Experience Manageable Failure

One of the most loving things parents can do is allow kids to experience manageable failure. That doesn't mean setting kids up to fail. It means not rescuing them from every consequence.

Forgetting a homework assignment.

Missing out on something because chores weren't done.

Feeling disappointed because money was spent too quickly.

These moments sting, but they teach. And they teach at a time when the cost is low and support is high. When kids aren't allowed to fail in childhood, they fail later in ways that are far more painful.

Failure, handled well, builds resilience. It teaches kids that mistakes aren't the end of the story. It builds problem-solving skills and emotional regulation. It creates humility. Avoiding failure doesn't build confidence. It builds fragility.

When Childhood Becomes a Performance

Another subtle shift that complicates parenting today is the way childhood has become performative. Kids are expected to achieve, excel, and stay busy. Parents feel pressure to curate the "right" experiences. Success becomes something to display rather than character to form.

In that environment, responsibility can feel like a distraction from success. Chores compete with activities. Work competes with performance.

Structure competes with flexibility. But adulthood does not reward performance without substance.

Character outlasts achievement.

Resilience outlasts talent.

Responsibility outlasts reputation.

When parents prioritize formation over performance, kids gain something far more durable.

Practicing Adulthood a Little at a Time

Preparing kids for adulthood doesn't require dramatic changes. It requires consistency.

Small responsibilities practiced daily.

Clear expectations held calmly.

Consequences that are predictable, not emotional.

Adults who model ownership and humility.

These things don't make headlines, but they shape lives. When kids grow up practicing adulthood in small ways, adulthood becomes less frightening and more manageable.

They know how to work.

They know how to wait.

They know how to handle disappointment.

They know how to contribute.

And perhaps most importantly, they learn to trust themselves.

Big Idea

Childhood is not meant to be a perfectly curated season of experiences; it is the training ground for adulthood. The goal of parenting is not simply to keep children happy or busy, but to prepare them to live well as adults. When children grow up with clear structure, meaningful responsibility, and the opportunity to experience manageable failure, they gradually develop competence, resilience, and ownership of their lives.

Structure is not the enemy of relationship, and responsibility is not the enemy of joy; both are essential to healthy development. By allowing children to practice adulthood in small, age-appropriate ways—learning to work, wait, contribute, and recover from mistakes—parents help them enter adulthood with confidence rather than overwhelm.

Looking Ahead

The chapters that follow will move from principle to practice.

We'll talk about how to structure responsibility in the home, how chores build shared ownership, how work and earning create dignity, how money teaches perspective, and how technology fits into all of it.

But all of that rests on this foundation: Childhood is practice for adulthood.

Structure is not the enemy of relationship. Responsibility is not the enemy of joy. They are the soil in which both grow.

Part 2

A Framework for Raising Grateful & Grounded Kids

Up to this point, we've explored the ideas behind privilege, responsibility, entitlement, and the culture we create in our homes. Beginning with chapter 6, we turn toward the practical work of putting those ideas into action.

This is where things move from theory to practice. And like most things that shape a family, the challenge is putting simple principles into practice consistently.

The chapters that follow focus on application. My goal is to show you how our family has tried to build rhythms of responsibility and healthy accountability around privileges—through technology planning, chores and work, and early financial stewardship—and the benefits we've experienced along the way.

You'll notice that some sections include a fair amount of detail. That's intentional. The principles themselves are simple, but applying them always happens within the unique culture of a family. Explaining how these practices work in our home—and how we've helped other families implement them—helps provide the context behind the ideas.

One thing that surprised me, as I've mentioned before, was how difficult it initially felt to create harmony around chores and technology boundaries. It seemed like these areas should have been simple to roll out and manage, yet we often found ourselves facing endless resistance.

Eventually we realized something important: The environment of our home—much like most homes today—was quietly structured in ways that resisted responsibility.

Many homes today are unintentionally structured to make privilege easy and responsibility optional. Changing that environment required real effort. But once the structure was in place and consistently upheld, maintaining it has not been nearly as difficult as we expected. So as you read the chapters that follow, you'll notice a fair amount of detail around developing plans and introducing them into your home. That's because there is an up-front investment. Some of these rhythms will likely be new, and they take intentional effort to establish.

The encouraging part is that once these systems are in place, the time required to maintain them tends to be relatively low, while the benefits are often quite significant.

At the same time, I've learned that the best setting for turning these ideas into a clear plan is rarely reading alone. In my experience, families gain the most clarity when they work through these principles together in seminars or workshops. In those environments, parents can ask questions, compare experiences, and thoughtfully adapt the framework to the culture of their own homes.

For many readers, this book simply serves as a starting point—an opportunity to consider the principles, evaluate whether they might be helpful for your family, and decide if you'd like to go further by developing a plan in a workshop or small-group setting. And if you've already participated in one of those gatherings, these chapters will likely serve as a helpful reminder of what we covered.

In many cases, workshops begin simply because one family finds the material helpful and invites others to explore it together. Churches, schools, and parent groups often host these gatherings so families can walk through the framework in community and begin developing plans for their own homes.

We begin part 2 with a focus on technology—a force that, in many homes, has become a significant source of disruption. This section is longer than the others because technology has become a complex and far-reaching part of family life. If you already feel confident in how your home approaches technology, feel free to skim ahead or jump directly to the final chapter on building a technology plan.

After that, we will explore how families can better understand why chores can be so difficult to upkeep and then develop a chores plan that brings order and shared responsibility into the home. From there we encourage kids to earn money and discover the value of work, learn to allocate what they earn, and begin building financial literacy that prepares them for adulthood.

Chapter 6

Technology and the Battle for Attention

Technology itself is not the enemy. It has expanded access to knowledge, strengthened communication across distance, and given children tools to learn, create, and explore the world in ways previous generations could not have imagined. Used well, technology can support learning, curiosity, and even connection.

But every good tool carries influence, and influence always requires wisdom. Technology is not neutral, and it does not simply sit in the background. It draws on our children's time and attention, often more quickly than we expect. This influence is present whether we are actively guiding or less aware, and it tends to fill open space with ease. In short, technology is forming our children when we are not looking.

The question is not whether technology is influencing our children, but rather what—or *who*—is winning their attention and shaping what they come to depend on.

The systems behind our screens are not designed to help children grow in self-regulation, patience, or meaningful relationship. Algorithms are engineered to capture attention, hold it, and then capture it again and again. They are optimized for engagement, not care. They do not know your child, value your child, or love your child—but they are very effective at convincing your child to keep coming back.

What begins as entertainment can quietly become reliance. And because technology is immersive, personalized, and always available, its influence often outpaces a parent's awareness. It does not knock. It moves in.

Scripture warns us that time and attention matter. As Paul wrote, "Be very careful, then, how you live—not as unwise but as wise, making the most of every opportunity, because the days are evil" (Ephesians 5:15–16 NIV). Our days are shaped by what holds our attention. When certain influences consistently win that space, they begin to shape what feels important, comforting, and worthy of our love.

Technology Is a Tool—But It Is a Very Influential Tool

Many parents are tempted to think of technology as a neutral tool—something that can be used well or poorly depending on the user. But this framing is incomplete. Technology has become a great tool because we have trained it to learn how we work.

That advantage can work for us or against us—and when the motivation behind the technology is revenue generation by big companies with shareholders to please, there is little incentive for them to design technology to have any primary motivation other than capturing our attention long enough to show us ads and sell us things.

Modern digital platforms are engineered to capture attention, remove stopping cues, and keep users engaged as long as possible. This is not accidental. It is the business model. As Andy and Amy Crouch observe in *My Tech-Wise Life*, our devices do not encourage occasional distraction; they train us into *a posture of distraction*. Over time, this posture reshapes what feels normal, tolerable, and satisfying.

This posture does not usually appear all at once. It develops slowly through small, repeated moments—checking a screen while waiting, scrolling during short breaks, reaching for a device at the first sign of boredom or discomfort. Over time, stillness begins to feel unfamiliar, silence feels empty, and attention becomes fragmented. Children may struggle to remain present in conversations, tasks, or play, not because they are unwilling, but because their attention has been trained to move quickly from one stimulus to the next. What once felt like ordinary waiting, wondering, or daydreaming is replaced by a constant pull toward distraction, and the body itself learns to stay slightly alert, slightly restless, always ready for the next interruption.

This posture of distraction is not limited to children. Adults experience the same pull toward interruption, novelty, and constant stimulation. The difference is not exposure, but timing. Their patterns of attention are actively taking shape, and the rhythms they practice now are becoming habits that will influence the rest of their lives. Because of this, children are especially vulnerable to influences that fragment attention or reward constant stimulation.

What Technology Is Teaching About Attention

Technology teaches children what is worth noticing.

Algorithms favor what is novel, emotionally charged, or extreme. Over time, this trains the brain to expect constant stimulation and to grow restless with silence, slowness, or ordinary moments.

Chris Fowler, a technology columnist for *The Washington Post* and previously *The Wall Street Journal*, wrote an article on how consumer technology is becoming increasingly driven by algorithms that prey on our deepest fears. "This is how the software driving Instagram, Facebook, TikTok, YouTube and lots of other apps has been designed to work," he writes. "Their algorithms optimize for eliciting a reaction from us, ignoring the fact that often the shortest path to a click is fear, anger or sadness."[24]

When we begin to lose the quiet war of our children's curiosity and creativity in life to the artificial world that stimulates easily behind the screen, we are sacrificing our kids' attention. Instead of developing tangible skills and values, they have become addicted to the cheap and curated thrill of technology's pull. We're all susceptible to this. Our kids' attention drifts away from people, toward content. And attention, over time, becomes love.

Erin Loechner writes,

> But in the digital world, there is no delicate balance. Fast-paced imagery and clamoring graphics plow through the boundary of boredom, crashing into overstimulation and, as a result, anxiety. "The bored self is conditioned to respond to the brightest, loudest, and most shocking volley for its attention," Dr. Kevin Gary explains to me. "Yet to sustain this constant stimulation, each arresting moment needs to be surpassed by yet another and another. The problem, then, is we do not ever cross the threshold which is the other side of boredom."[25]

Every swipe, click, and tap trains the brain to expect novelty and reward. Dopamine is released not only when something pleasurable is experienced, but when it is *anticipated*. The result is a restless search for the next hit—another video, another message, another update.

Last year, I concluded that I needed to delete Instagram from my phone. For a long time, I could jump on for a few minutes and jump off without much issue. But over time, the algorithm learned me—too well. I found myself intending to check one thing and resurfacing much later, having accomplished nothing except a vague sense that time had disappeared.

I didn't delete Instagram because of inappropriate content or obvious abuse. I deleted it because I noticed something subtler: Every time I finished scrolling, I felt more bored than when I started. Not rested. Not refreshed. Just slightly depleted.

If I picked up my phone to read the news, that was usually fine. But Instagram was different. It was too enjoyable. Too tailored. It knew exactly how to keep me engaged. A quick video of an old car from the 1990s being restored in sixty seconds. Someone tearing apart a car stereo. Backyard explosions. Fishing clips. Hockey goals. Financial hot takes. Video of an electrician doing electrical work. All the greatest hits of mildly interesting, mostly unnecessary content—served up endlessly.

And then, just often enough to keep things "interesting," a subtly sexualized video would slip in. Same type of content, different packaging. A trades video—but now the focus wasn't the trades work, it was the unusually pretty, young woman doing it. I wasn't asking for it. I wasn't hearting other messages like it to signal Instagram's algorithm to send me more. But it kept coming anyway. The novelty wasn't the skill; it was the distraction.

That's when it clicked for me. If Instagram knows this much about a forty-two-year-old man who's trying to be thoughtful and restrained, how precisely do you think it understands a thirteen-year-old boy? Or a thirteen-year-old girl? And how much harder is it for them to notice what's happening while it's happening?

Ecclesiastes names this reality with unsettling clarity: "The eye is not satisfied with seeing, nor the ear filled with hearing" (1:8). Desire, when fed without limits, doesn't settle; it stretches.

Boredom has quietly become a threat in modern homes—not because boredom is harmful, but because we no longer tolerate it. Boredom is not a condition to eliminate. It is the space where imagination wakes up. It is where children learn to create meaning rather than consume it. The issue isn't that technology is entertaining. It's that it is exceptionally good at holding attention—and our children are still developing the discernment to notice when something is shaping them.

And if I'm honest, I am not immune. When I finally have downtime, I want relief. Mental quiet. A break. That desire is understandable.

But if I instinctively reach for distraction the moment I feel fatigue, I shouldn't be surprised when my kids do the same. Boredom is not a childhood weakness; it is a human discomfort. And the question is not whether we need rest. We do. The question is what kind of rest we are choosing—escape or restoration.

Sometimes the impulse to scroll is less about rest and more about overload. It may be a signal that life is too crowded. Breaks are good and naps are wonderful. But bouncing between email, weather, texts, news alerts, and notifications is not rest. It is stimulation disguised as relief.

The challenge is that this behavior is encouraged. It feels harmless. It feels productive. It feels normal. But what is easy is rarely formative. And what trains us trains our children.

Clicking for Updates . . . Refresh, Refresh, Refresh

When attention is repeatedly pulled toward the wrong things, children don't just become distracted; they begin to draw the wrong conclusions about what matters. Attention is not merely a spotlight; it is a filter. Whatever consistently holds it begins to feel important, valuable, and worthy of pursuit. Over time, children come to conclusions not because they were taught them explicitly, but because their attention was quietly trained in a particular direction.

This is where the concern deepens. When a child's attention is dominated by what is fast, flashy, emotionally charged, or endlessly entertaining, they begin to assume that these qualities define what is meaningful. Subtlety feels boring. Effort feels unnecessary. Ordinary moments feel empty. The conclusion is not stated out loud, but it is learned all the same: *If it doesn't grab me immediately, it's probably not worth my time.*

This shaping of attention does not happen only through social media or obvious algorithmic feeds. It also happens through the shows children stream, the pace and tone of commercials, and the rhythm of modern entertainment itself. Many shows are designed to move quickly, resolve tension instantly, and roll seamlessly into the next episode. Commercials are engineered to interrupt attention with urgency, novelty, or desire. Even "harmless" content often trains children to expect constant stimulation and rapid payoff, leaving them less equipped to engage with activities that require patience, persistence, or quiet focus.

Just as important, distraction today often shows up not as exposure to extreme content, but as **constant switching**. A child moves from a school-issued laptop to a phone, from a phone to a tablet, from a tablet to the television. While a show plays in the background, they check messages. While homework is open, notifications interrupt. They respond to a text, open a game, glance at email, scroll briefly, then return to the original task—only to repeat the cycle again minutes later. Nothing feels especially harmful in isolation. The problem is the pattern.

As Jonathan Haidt observes in *The Anxious Generation*, "The phone-based life, in contrast, is a never-ending series of notifications, alerts, and distractions, fragmenting consciousness and training us to fill every moment of consciousness with something from our phones."[26]

This kind of fragmented attention trains the brain to stay slightly unsettled, always alert for the next interruption. Focus becomes shallow. Presence becomes difficult. Instead of learning how to stay with one thing—an idea, a conversation, a task—children learn how to bounce. Over time, this bouncing can shape how they understand learning, relationships, and even themselves. Life begins to feel like something to manage quickly rather than inhabit fully.

I have gotten to the point where we take time to explain to our kids how important it is for them to be bored, and how discovering things to do other than screens and video games is so healthy for the brain.

One time, I explained to them that it's okay to have screens and tech in moderation, just like sugar and candy. But if all we did was eat Mike and Ike's for breakfast, lunch, and dinner, eventually our bodies would wear out and we would develop major health problems. Mike and Ike's aren't meant to be consumed for a living; they are a treat. Too much sugar isn't good for our bodies.

Boredom is the fruits and vegetables of psychological development. It's what we need, but rarely do we want it. Usually we want the quick fix, but deep down we know we need something more wholesome—just less fun.

If you set out two bowls on the counter—one filled with candy, the other with fruit—and told your kids they were free to eat as much as they wanted, which bowl would empty first? And if you kept refilling it, how long would the fruit last in comparison?

Technology and screens often work the same way. They can function like sugar for the brain—fast, stimulating, and immediately rewarding. In moderation, it can be enjoyable. But as a steady diet, it's not healthy—especially for developing children. The problem isn't that technology is inherently bad; it's that it's extraordinarily difficult to self-regulate. Left unchecked, it crowds out slower, more nourishing experiences that actually build attention, patience, and resilience.

Technology and the Formation of Identity

Technology doesn't just shape what children do; it quietly shapes who they believe they are.

Social platforms turn visibility into value. Likes, views, followers, streaks, and comments quantify attention and attach it to identity. Over time, children can begin to associate worth with performance and approval rather than character, contribution, and belonging.

Research reflects this tension. Studies consistently show that younger generations deeply crave authenticity and connection, yet are increasingly shaped by comparison and anxiety. Technology intensifies that contradiction by offering constant feedback without the stability of embodied relationship.

One teenager quoted in *The Opt-Out Family* captured this confusion with remarkable honesty:

> "I know [influencers] aren't really my friends," says one teen I spoke with. "But also, they kind of are? Like, they share stuff that my friends don't or won't talk to me about, so in a way, I'm closer with [influencers] than with the people I know in real life."[27]

This statement reveals the subtle danger: **Technology can simulate intimacy while quietly replacing it.**

Today's children, especially those on social media, inhabit an environment where validation is constant, curated, and scalable—and where even artificial or fabricated content can feel compelling. The volume and velocity have changed, and with them, the pressures placed on developing identity.

When identity is formed around attention rather than belonging, approval rather than contribution, children are left anxious, comparing, and uncertain—always visible, but not always known.

When Formation Happens Apart from Relationship

One of the quieter ways technology shapes children is not through what it shows them, but through **how it engages them—largely apart from relationship**. Much of a child's digital life unfolds alone. Possibly physically alone, and also relationally unaccompanied. What they see, hear, search, and absorb often happens without a trusted adult nearby to help them interpret what is taking place.

This shaping extends far beyond social media. It includes the things children search for when they feel insecure or curious and don't know who else to ask. It includes the constant stream of group texts, side chats, and message threads where tone is flattened, misunderstandings multiply, and social pressure quietly circulates. It includes the language children hear while playing live video games—trash talk from strangers, sarcasm from friends, insults passed off as humor.

What makes this different from most formative experiences is that it happens **without guidance**. When children encounter confusing or unhealthy messages in real-world relationships, there is often a parent, teacher, or mentor nearby to notice, intervene, or at least provide context. In digital spaces, children are left to interpret things on their own. They draw conclusions about what is normal, acceptable, or expected without anyone helping them sort truth from noise.

At the same time, technology rarely feels impersonal to children. Algorithms surface personalities—real and artificial—at every turn. Influencers, streamers, commenters, advertisements, and anonymous voices all speak into a child's world with familiarity and confidence. Over time, this creates the sense that someone is always present, always responding, always available. Technology begins to feel relational, even when it is not accountable, invested, or trustworthy.

The influence of social media on youth identity has become a growing concern among researchers and educators. As Molly Smith explains, young people often measure their worth through the feedback they receive online: "The proliferation of social media has also fueled the need for validation and social approval among young people. The number of likes, comments, and followers has become a measure of self-worth, amplifying the pressure to present an idealized version of oneself online."[28]

This is why it is easy to underestimate how deeply technology shapes children. From the outside, it looks like entertainment, communication, or passing time. From the inside, it often feels like connection, affirmation, or belonging. And because so much of this engagement happens quietly, privately, and repeatedly, it forms assumptions long before parents realize there is anything to address.

The concern is not that children encounter voices beyond the family. The concern is that these voices now arrive **constantly, unfiltered, and unaccompanied**, shaping language, expectations, humor, values, and self-understanding without relational context. Children are left to carry the weight of interpretation alone.

When formation happens apart from relationship, it tends to be louder, faster, and less discerning. Reclaiming relational presence—conversation, guidance, shared reflection—is not about control. It is about ensuring that children are not left alone to make sense of a world that is speaking to them from every direction.

David Tucker rightly notes in *The Digital Parenting Guidebook* that digital parenting is a form of discipleship. If parents do not actively shape this space, formation does not stop; it is simply outsourced.

Technology is always willing to step in.

Modeling Is the Loudest Lesson

As with money, what parents model matters more than what they mandate. Children notice interruptions. They notice divided attention. Long before children understand rules or restrictions, they are watching patterns. They notice what draws our attention, what interrupts us, and what we return to when we are tired, bored, or stressed. What we practice in ordinary moments quietly teaches our children what is normal.

Modeling is not optional. It *is* the curriculum. If parents cannot put phones down, boundaries will feel hollow.

Telling a child to limit screen time while regularly checking our phones during conversations, meals, or downtime sends a mixed message. Children are remarkably perceptive. They learn not only from what we say about technology, but from how we live with it. Over time, they internalize what appears to hold the highest claim on our presence.

Modeling healthy behavior does not require perfection. It requires visibility and consistency. When children see parents put phones away during conversations, choose rest without screens, or resist the impulse to fill every quiet moment with noise, they are learning a healthy model of behavior.

Parents also model how to respond when technology becomes too much. Naming our own limits—"I need to put this down," or "I've noticed this is distracting me"—helps children understand that self-regulation is a skill practiced over time, not a trait some people simply possess.

Just as important, modeling creates permission for conversation. When parents are willing to reflect openly on their own habits, children are more likely to share what they are experiencing online. They learn that questions, confusion, and even mistakes can be brought into relationship rather than hidden. This relational safety is one of the most powerful protective factors a family can offer.

Healthy habits around technology are not built primarily through monitoring software or rigid rules, but through shared rhythms. Eating meals without devices. Watching shows together rather than separately. Reading, resting, or working in ways that demonstrate sustained attention. These practices teach children that focus is not merely expected of them; it is something the whole household values.

One peer-reviewed research found that children tend to adopt the habits they see modeled most often. As one large cross-national study concluded, "Children tend to share their parents' reading attitudes and behaviors."[29] Shocking, I know.

And, sometimes how we interact with our own phone gives our kids an impression we would prefer to be made aware of. In *The Opt-Out Family*, Erin Loechner writes the following:

> A Louisiana elementary-school teacher recently witnessed a striking similarity in her classroom. After she gave the class a writing prompt, four of her students told her they wished phones had never been invented. Wrote one student, "I don't like the phone because my [parents] are on their phone every day. . . . I hate my mom's phone and I wish she never had one."[30]

It seems that kids aren't necessarily glad for smart phones when it comes to their parents. In a world where attention is constantly pulled outward, parental modeling quietly draws it back home. It reminds children that presence is possible, that limits are life-giving, and that learning how to live well with technology begins not with restriction, but with example.

Technology Is Here to Stay

Technology is not going away. Probably the opposite in many ways.

The goal is not to raise children who fear screens or reject them entirely. The goal is to raise children who know how to place technology in its proper role—as a tool, not a treasure.

When we don't pay attention to what's shaping us, it ends up shaping us anyway. But when we're intentional—setting boundaries and staying present—those same influences can serve us rather than compete with us.

That is stewardship. And it is how we prepare our children to live wisely—and faithfully—in a digital age.

Artificial Intelligence (AI) and Childhood

One of the central concerns with many modern technologies—including artificial intelligence—is not simply what they show our children, but what they *remove*. Increasingly, technology is designed to take the struggle out of work. It shortens the path, smooths the friction, and delivers outcomes with minimal effort. While this efficiency can be helpful in some contexts, it carries a real cost during childhood and adolescence.

And this is especially true of artificial intelligence.

Struggle is not an obstacle to development; it is the pathway through which development happens. Wrestling with a difficult idea, pushing through frustration, sitting with uncertainty, and learning how to persist when progress is slow—these experiences are formative. They build resilience, patience, creativity, and confidence. They shape personality. They teach children not just *how* to do something, but who they are becoming as they do it.

Artificial intelligence does not eliminate struggle altogether, but it changes its nature. The struggle shifts from doing the work to deciding what to ask, how to prompt, or how to refine outputs. That is a different kind of effort—often more abstract and less emotionally demanding.

For adults with a formed sense of self and responsibility, this shift may be appropriate. For children who are still learning how to think, write, reason, and persist, it can quietly bypass essential developmental work.

The danger is not that children use helpful tools; it is that tools begin to replace the very challenges that grow them. When writing becomes something generated rather than composed, when problem-solving becomes something outsourced rather than practiced, and when discomfort is quickly avoided rather than endured, children miss opportunities to develop internal strength. What looks like competence on the surface may mask a lack of confidence underneath.

From adolescence through high school, children are meant to encounter struggle. They are meant to experience effort that does not immediately pay off, confusion that requires time, and tasks that stretch them beyond what feels comfortable. These struggles teach children that they can endure difficulty without escaping it, that their voice matters even when it is imperfect, and that growth often happens slowly.

This is not an argument against technology or AI. It is an argument for discernment. There may be moments when artificial intelligence supports learning and moments when it undermines it. The guiding question for parents is not *Does this make things easier?* but *Does this remove the kind of struggle my child still needs?*

We do not want our children spared from all difficulty. We want them shaped by the right kinds of difficulty. Character is not formed by frictionless progress, but by learning to stay present when something is hard. In a world increasingly designed to eliminate struggle, parents play a crucial role in preserving the kinds of challenges that help children become resilient, capable, and grounded adults.

Big Idea

Technology is not just a tool our children use; it is a teacher that is quietly forming their attention, identity, and sense of belonging.

When left unchecked or unexamined, it trains distraction, replaces embodied relationship, and shapes desire in ways that undermine formation. When engaged intentionally—within limits and loving presence—it can be shaped to serve, rather than compete with, what matters most.

20 Key Takeaways

1. Technology is formative, not neutral.
2. Digital systems are designed to capture attention and keep it. Their

primary goal is engagement, not care, and their influence is present whether parents are actively guiding or not.

3. Attention is a moral and formative reality.
4. What repeatedly captures a child's attention begins to shape what feels important, valuable, and worthy of love. Over time, attention becomes affection.
5. The greatest danger is not only extreme content, but fragmented attention.
6. Constant switching—between devices, apps, notifications, and screens—trains restlessness, shallow focus, and difficulty with presence, even when no single interaction feels harmful.
7. Boredom is not the enemy; it is formative.
8. Boredom creates the space where imagination, creativity, resilience, and self-direction develop. Technology is exceptionally good at eliminating boredom—and in doing so, it crowds out growth.
9. Technology shapes identity by turning visibility into value.
10. Likes, views, streaks, and followers attach worth to performance and approval rather than character, contribution, and belonging. This fosters anxiety, comparison, and fragile self-understanding.
11. Digital spaces often form children apart from relationship.
12. Much of a child's online life unfolds without adult guidance, leaving them to interpret meaning, values, and norms alone—while algorithms and anonymous voices speak with confidence and frequency.
13. Simulated intimacy can quietly replace real belonging.
14. Influencers, streamers, and online communities can feel relational without being mutual, accountable, or committed—leaving children visible but not deeply known.
15. Parents are the most powerful formative influence through modeling.
16. What parents practice around attention teaches more loudly than what they mandate. Children notice what consistently wins their parents' focus.
17. Healthy technology habits are built through shared rhythms, not just rules.
18. Presence, conversation, device-free meals, and modeling restraint teach children that attention can be directed rather than surrendered.
19. Technology will always step in if parents do not.
20. Formation does not stop in the absence of guidance; it is simply outsourced to systems that do not know or love the child.

Chapter 7

Managing Technology in the Home—Part 1

In the previous chapter, we explored how technology quietly reshapes attention, desire, and posture—often without our awareness. That work was diagnostic by design. Before families can respond wisely, they must first see clearly what is happening beneath the surface. This chapter assumes that groundwork. The focus now shifts from *what technology is doing* to *how families can govern it well.*

Most families don't struggle with technology because they lack rules. They struggle because they lack conviction. Rules without shared conviction feel arbitrary. Plans without principles feel fragile. And when pressure comes—from tired evenings, comparison with peers, or children who push back—families often retreat to reaction instead of intention.

New devices, new platforms, new social norms, and now artificial intelligence arrive faster than any single rulebook can keep up with. What families need first is not a perfect plan, but a clear framework—a set of guiding principles that help parents decide *why* they do what they do before they decide *how* to do it.

This chapter is a countdown of convictions. Each topic addresses a different layer of family life around technology: environment, authority, development, relationship, and responsibility. Some topics will feel practical and concrete. Others will feel more foundational and relational. Technology does not affect one narrow area of life; it touches everything from attention and identity to belonging and discipline.

The goal of this chapter is not to convince families to reject technology or fear it. It is to help parents place technology in its proper role, so it serves the life of the family rather than reshaping it. The chapter that follows will translate these topics into a clear, workable technology plan—but plans only hold when families know what they're protecting and why it matters.

We begin with the most visible, least relational aspects of family technology use—and move steadily toward the most formative.

This is like your ESPN Top 10 Technology Topics countdown—from Doug's perspective. I'll say, as important as the first eight are, it's really the top two that carry the day. This chapter will hit numbers 6 to 10. (The next chapter includes the top five.)

Here are the topics we will cover in this chapter:

#10 – TV Streaming and YouTube
#9 – Isolate Technology to Its Primary Use
#8 – Technology Ownership
#7 – Friends of Your Kids and Sleepovers
#6 – Phones

#10 – TV Streaming and YouTube

When Nothing Ever Stops, Parents Must

For many families, television streaming and YouTube feel relatively harmless. There is no direct interaction with strangers and no pressure to perform. And yet, these platforms often exert more influence over the emotional tone of a home than parents expect.

Beyond having age-appropriate profiles set up for your kids to use that filter out inappropriate content (hopefully!), this topic is focused on *how* the streaming practically functions in the mind of a child.

The central issue is not simply what children watch, but **how watching is designed to work**. Modern streaming platforms remove natural stopping points. Episodes autoplay. Recommendations appear instantly. One video flows seamlessly into the next. The environment itself is built to keep attention engaged for as long as possible.

For adults, this often feels like lost time. For children, it becomes formative. Children are still learning how to regulate attention and emotion. When entertainment never ends on its own, they do not practice stopping. They learn to remain immersed until something external interrupts them.

Parents recognize the pattern: A child seems calm while watching, then becomes irritable or restless when screen time ends. This is frequently misread as defiance. **More often, it is overstimulation**. Fast-paced visuals and emotional intensity flood the nervous system. When the screen turns off, the body struggles to recalibrate.

YouTube intensifies this dynamic. Unlike traditional television, YouTube is not just a library; it is an algorithmic feed. Content is selected to maximize engagement, not suitability. Over time, novelty escalates because novelty keeps viewers watching. Even age-appropriate content can train the brain to expect constant stimulation.

The danger is subtle but real. Silence begins to feel uncomfortable. Slowness feels boring. Ordinary activities—conversation, reading, unstructured play—struggle to compete.

As Adam Alter, author of *Irresistible: The Rise of Addictive Technology and the Business of Keeping Us Hooked*, writes, "Companies have systematically removed stopping cues—those brief moments . . . that suggest you might want to move on to something else."[31]

Children are not failing when they struggle to disengage. They are responding exactly as the environment invites them to respond.

This is why families must provide what the platforms will not: **limits that create stopping points**. This does not require eliminating screens. It requires containing them. Clear boundaries around when, where, and how long screens are used protect children from systems designed never to stop.

When nothing ever stops naturally, parents must decide when enough is enough.

Summary: Why This Topic Matters

- Streaming platforms are engineered for continuous engagement.
- Children lack the capacity to stop themselves consistently.
- Overstimulation increases dysregulation.
- The concern is not content alone, but endless consumption.
- Parents must provide the stopping points technology removes.

#9 – Isolate Technology to Its Primary Use

Clarity of Purpose Reduces Conflict and Confusion

Modern devices are marketed for versatility. Phones, tablets, and computers can do nearly everything the others can. What begins as convenience quickly becomes confusion. When a single device serves many purposes, boundaries blur and conflict multiplies.

Parents find themselves constantly negotiating intent: *Is this for school or for fun? Is this necessary or optional?* Children learn to toggle between uses faster than parents can track. Expectations become unclear, and enforcement becomes exhausting.

"I have time on my computer" can mean a lot more than homework. "You said I could play video games," but now your child is watching YouTube on their Nintendo Switch.

Isolating technology to its primary use restores order.

A television is for shows and movies.

A gaming console is for games.

A computer is for schoolwork and research.

A phone is for communication.

You pick your own boundaries; those are what ours look like. Phones and computers are the toughest, because their potential is just sitting idly there. Once you open up the access to new features of the device, it's hard to take them back.

When devices are limited to their intended function, the environment communicates the boundary. Enforcement becomes simpler because expectations are visible and consistent.

Tablets often present the greatest challenge. Unlike phones or computers, they rarely have a clear primary purpose, which makes them especially difficult to govern. Portable and private, they tend to drift away from shared spaces and into corners of the house, under blankets, or behind closed doors. Unless carefully restricted, they can quickly become the most distracting device in the home.

For that reason, we no longer allow tablets. We did at one time, but over time I grew uncomfortable with how they were being used. Even with parental controls in place, the posture of tablet use—isolated, inward-facing, and detached—worked against the kind of presence and accountability we were trying to cultivate. I personally have a tablet because it's where I do most of my reading, but my kids are not allowed to use it.

Over time, I came to a simple conclusion: There wasn't much our kids could do on a tablet that I wouldn't rather see them do on a device with a clearer purpose and more defined boundaries. Educational apps make sense in theory. But in practice, that wasn't how tablets were being used in our home. They drifted toward entertainment, distraction, and low-friction consumption.

That's our experience—not a universal rule. If tablets serve meaningful, intentional purposes in your home, that may be a different story. Technology is far easier to manage when its role is narrow and visible. When a device has a clear purpose, it becomes a tool again—not a default environment.

Isolating the Purpose of Phones

As a side note, the device most prone to misuse in the home is the smartphone. A modern smartphone holds more power and potential than all the consumer technology combined available just a couple decades ago—and that power matters most when placed in the hands of a developing child.

The central problem is not that phones have a primary purpose, but that they are allowed to become endlessly multifunctional. Children have time, curiosity, and boredom working in their favor. When a phone can do everything, they will explore everything—testing boundaries, downloading new apps, joining group threads with people they may or may not know, and justifying it all under the simple claim, "It's my phone time."

Phones also quietly demand privacy. The more functions a phone serves—communication, entertainment, browsing, social interaction—the more personal it begins to feel. And the more personal it feels, the less open children tend to be to parental review. What begins as a tool slowly shifts into something they believe belongs solely to them.

When a phone can do anything and everything, it stops being a tool and becomes something altogether different. Isolating its purpose helps children relate to it appropriately—and helps parents retain clarity, authority, and trust.

Summary: Why This Topic Matters

- Multipurpose devices blur boundaries and increase conflict.
- Isolating technology by function simplifies expectations and enforcement.
- Tablets require special caution due to their lack of purpose clarity.
- Healthy friction supports attention and self-regulation.

#8 – Technology Ownership

Why Parents Must Remain the IT Department of the Home

One of the most quietly formative questions in family technology management is also one of the most easily overlooked: **Who owns the technology?**

Many families answer this question without ever naming it. Devices are given as gifts, earned through allowance, or framed as milestones. A tablet becomes personal property. A laptop feels "theirs." And once ownership shifts, posture shifts with it.

Children relate very differently to what they believe they own versus what they are allowed to use. Ownership carries entitlement. Stewardship carries responsibility. When a device is owned, limits feel intrusive. When a device is issued, limits feel expected.

This distinction explains much of the tension families experience around screens.

When technology is framed as a gift or rite of passage, it quietly moves from **tool** to **treasure**. *This is mine now.* Later restrictions feel arbitrary or unfair—not because parents are unreasonable, but because authority has subtly changed. Parents may still hold formal authority, but relational authority has already begun to erode.

This is why ownership must be clear from the beginning.

I often explain it this way: **Parents are the IT department of the home**. Just as employees don't bring their own servers into the office or install whatever software they want on company machines, children should not be the final authority over powerful tools that affect the whole system.

Technology in the home should be

- issued intentionally,
- configured with purpose,
- reviewed regularly, and
- adjusted as maturity grows.

This framing also removes unnecessary conflict. When parents retain ownership, boundaries don't feel personal. They feel structural. Limits are not punishments; they are policies. Access is not assumed; it is earned and revisited.

This matters especially when children want to purchase their own devices. Encouraging work ethic is good. Teaching responsibility through earning is good. But some tools are simply too formative to be privately owned during childhood.

Allowing a child to buy and "own" their own device—particularly a phone or computer—often transfers authority before the child is ready to carry it. Even when rules are verbally agreed upon, the internal logic shifts: *I paid for this. It belongs to me.*

That shift makes future guidance far harder than it needs to be.

Retaining ownership does not prevent independence; it paces it. Devices can gain functionality over time. Restrictions can loosen gradually. Conversations can deepen. Freedom can grow alongside demonstrated maturity.

Ownership is not a technical detail in technology management. It sets the tone for authority, responsibility, and trust. When parents remain the IT department—clear, calm, and consistent—technology stays in its proper place as a tool that serves the family rather than reorganizing it.

Summary: Why This Topic Matters

- Ownership shapes posture; stewardship shapes responsibility.
- When children believe they own devices, limits feel intrusive.
- Retaining parental ownership preserves authority and clarity.
- Parents function best as the IT department of the home.

#7 – Friends of Your Kids and Sleepovers

Why Peer Environments Multiply What You Allow at Home

No matter how thoughtfully a family manages technology within their own walls, children do not live only at home. Friends, teammates, classmates, and neighbors all bring their own devices, habits, and expectations with them. And it is often in these peer environments that technology exposure accelerates most quickly.

Sleepovers, playdates, and team gatherings are **multiplier moments**. A single device can introduce content, language, or experiences that would never occur in your home. Parents sometimes assume that boundaries naturally travel with their child. In reality, those boundaries often soften—or disappear—the moment a child enters a different environment.

This is not a critique of other parents. Families are navigating different values, pressures, and levels of awareness. The issue here is not judgment; it is **preparation**.

Sleepovers, in particular, carry a unique vulnerability. When adults go to bed, screens tend to come out. Phones slip under blankets. Group chats intensify. YouTube queues form. Language shifts. What feels manageable during the day can become something very different late at night.

Children who are unprepared for these moments are left to navigate them alone. They may feel awkward enforcing boundaries they didn't choose. They may fear exclusion. Or they may simply go along, even when something doesn't sit right.

This is why healthy technology management extends beyond household rules. Children need clarity about what is expected of them when they are away from home.

Talking with Other Parents (It's Usually Easier Than You Think)

Parents also benefit from direct, simple communication with other parents. A short conversation before a sleepover—"Here's how we handle devices at home [or at night]. How do you guys usually navigate devices at home [or at night]?"—often brings relief rather than tension.

In my experience, most parents are not opposed to clear boundaries around technology in shared spaces. In fact, many are relieved that someone is willing to name them first. No one wants to be the "bad guy," and many parents are quietly unsure where to draw the line themselves. Your clarity often gives them permission to borrow your approach, at least temporarily.

These conversations do not need to be long or loaded. Calm, matter-of-fact communication goes a long way. Clarity builds trust.

When Other Kids Bring Technology into Your Home

This principle works in both directions. Just as your children enter other homes, other children bring their devices into yours. This is why it's important for parents to know their own guidelines clearly—and to communicate them with confidence.

When kids come into your home, they are entering *your* environment. That means your expectations apply. Phones don't need to be confiscated dramatically, but it is entirely appropriate to say things like

- "We keep phones in common areas."
- "Devices get turned in at bedtime."
- "We don't do scrolling on YouTube or social media."

Children adjust quickly when expectations are clear and consistently applied. Confusion—and conflict—arises far more often when rules are vague or inconsistently enforced.

Knowing your guidelines ahead of time allows you to lead calmly rather than reactively. It also removes pressure from your child, who no longer has to negotiate boundaries on your behalf.

Peer Pressure Requires Empathy, Not Surrender

Understanding peer pressure helps parents respond wisely. "Everyone else can" is not a moral argument; it is a social one. Belonging matters deeply to children, especially as they grow older.

Recognizing this allows parents to hold boundaries without dismissing their child's desire to belong. Empathy keeps the relationship intact; clarity keeps the boundary intact.

Friends matter. Belonging matters. But belonging should never require exposure to everything peers allow. Helping children navigate peer environments with confidence—both inside and outside your home—is one of the most protective gifts parents can offer.

Summary: Why This Topic Matters

- Peer environments often expand technology exposure quickly.
- Sleepovers introduce risks that daytime use does not.
- Children need preparation, not just rules, for other homes.
- Clear expectations reduce pressure and confusion—for everyone involved.
- Parent-to-parent communication is usually welcomed, not resisted.
- Knowing and communicating your own home guidelines protects both kids and relationships.

#6 – Phones

Why the Most Powerful Device Requires the Most Caution

No piece of technology reshapes childhood more decisively than the smartphone.

Phones are different not only because they are portable, but because they are **personal**. A television belongs to a room. A computer usually belongs to a shared space. A smartphone belongs to a pocket. It follows a child everywhere—into bedrooms, friendships, boredom, anxiety, and moments of loneliness. It becomes a constant companion.

That alone should give parents pause.

Many families approach phones primarily through the lens of convenience or safety: *I want to be able to reach them. They're walking home. What if I'm late for pickup. Everyone else has one.* These concerns are understandable and often legitimate. But they rarely account for what a smartphone introduces beyond communication.

A smartphone is not simply a phone. It is a portal—into entertainment, private messaging, comparison, infinite information, and algorithm-driven content. Giving a child a smartphone without carefully limiting its function can have real consequences.

This is why the question is not simply *when* a child gets a phone, but **what kind of phone** they are given. There is a meaningful difference between a device designed primarily for calling and texting and one capable of streaming, gaming, browsing, posting, and messaging at all hours. Those differences shape attention, expectations, emotional regulation, and social pressure.

Many parents discover this only after the fact. A phone is introduced with good intentions and reasonable rules, but the device itself invites more than rules can realistically contain. Parents find themselves stuck in constant reaction—adjusting settings, monitoring behavior, negotiating access, responding to situations they never anticipated.

Children are not failing when this happens. Smartphones are extraordinarily effective at capturing attention. Adults struggle with this. Expecting children to manage it independently places adult-level responsibility on developing brains.

This is why many experts encourage delaying smartphones as long as possible and, when communication is genuinely needed, choosing devices that are intentionally limited. Movements like Wait Until 8th reflect a growing consensus: the concern is not communication itself, but **early access to fully equipped smartphones**. Even then, the strongest caution applies to phones without meaningful parental controls.

There is also a relational cost to early, unrestricted phone access that often goes unnoticed. When children have constant private communication, parents lose natural points of conversation. Instead of processing social dynamics aloud, children retreat inward. Confusion goes unshared. Parents often learn about problems only after they have grown more complex.

Unlike other devices, a smartphone promises independence, connection, and competence all at once. To a child, it feels like the gateway into the adult world. And once a child sets their heart on that gateway, something fascinating happens.

This is why phones so quickly become the Precious. If they don't have it, and they begin to really want it, this is where they suddenly become long-game, thoughtful salespeople who will "win over" their parents at all costs, on their parents' terms.

They become excellent negotiators.

Suddenly, they're Zig Ziglar.

Their arguments grow thoughtful.

Their tone becomes measured.

Their patience is remarkable.

They stop demanding and start strategizing. They remember things you said weeks ago and bring them back at just the right time. They play the long game.

You'll hear

- "I've really been thinking about this."
- "I understand your concerns."
- "I'm not asking now—just eventually."
- "I've been really responsible lately."

And honestly—you'll be impressed. This is not evidence that your child is suddenly ready. It is evidence that **desire sharpens focus.**

In *The Lord of the Rings*, the Precious doesn't rush in or overpower; it simply draws the eye. It becomes the thing that feels most interesting, most important, most worth holding on to. Smartphones work in much the same way for kids. They are the newest and coolest thing their friends are getting, the thing adults seem to carry everywhere, the small object that promises entry into a bigger world. And little by little, attention bends toward it, until other interests quietly lose their pull.

This is where parents must distinguish persuasion from readiness.

A child may sound mature. They may argue well. They may genuinely believe they are ready. But readiness for persuasion or ownership is not the same as readiness for exposure. Phones introduce private communication, constant comparison, algorithmic content, and fragmented attention—often all at once.

A simple diagnostic helps clarify this: **If a device requires constant surveillance to remain safe, it likely exceeds a child's capacity**.

Phones are not harmful by nature. They are powerful. And powerful tools should be introduced slowly, with clarity and limits, during a season when parents are still meant to govern heavily. The iPhone should never be the Precious.

When phones are treated as tools rather than milestones, children are spared unnecessary pressure and parents retain the ability to guide wisely. Over time, access can grow—but only as maturity, discernment, and self-control grow with it. That is not restriction. That is stewardship.

There are many options that meet communication needs without opening the full digital ecosystem. Gabb and Bark phones are app-limited smartphones by design. Apple Watches and Gabb watches are excellent entry points, proving an important point: the primary function of a phone is communication.

That's how we approached it in our home. We started with Gabb phones. Later, we experimented with a tightly locked-down iPhone—no search capability, no app downloads, screen-time limits, filtered music content. It worked, but only because we put in the time to set it up, monitor it, and maintain it.

Our other kids won't get a smartphone at that age. We'll likely use a watch instead.

There is much more that could be said, but for the purposes of this chapter, this is the core conviction: **Your child does not need the newest phone**. What they need is clarity, consistency, and parents with the resolve to hold the line—even when your child suddenly becomes Grant Cardone in their sales pitch.

Most requests for a phone are framed around communication, and that need can be met without opening the door to everything else. There is no reason you can't provide a phone or smartwatch that allows your child to call and text—without social media, apps, or constant distraction. You don't have to cave to the demand simply because it's common or culturally expected.

Yes, holding that boundary may feel harsh in the moment. But it's part of your responsibility in shepherding your child's development. Limits are not a failure of love; they are one of its most important expressions.

Summary: Why This Topic Matters

- Phones are personal, portable, and uniquely immersive.
- Smartphones introduce far more than communication.
- Children lack the developmental capacity to self-regulate phone use consistently.
- Readiness for persuasion is not readiness for exposure.
- Delayed and limited access protects attention, relationships, and emotional health.

By understanding some of the most important topics around technology, parents will save themselves and their kids from a lot of unnecessary conflicts and exposure. Technology isn't a small thing, it is a gateway into the world that your kids are not likely ready for. Being able to identify your kids' maturity, the primary purpose of different kinds of technology, and being ready to have limits right away (that can be adjusted over time and context) sets you up to succeed in the home. This is the opposite of handicapping your kids—that is, waiting to introduce varying levels of technology until they (and you) are ready for it.

Chapter 8

Managing Technology in the Home—Part 2

Let's now move to the top five "managing technology" topics according to Doug:

#5 – Social Media

#4 – Parental Controls

#3 – Unstructured Play and the Non-Tech Environment

#2 – Parents' Examples and Attitudes

#1 – Prevention and Ongoing Conversation

#5 – Social Media

Why Identity and Comparison Arrive Too Early

If phones change the structure of a child's day, **social media reshapes how a child understands themselves.**

Social media platforms are not neutral tools for connection. They are systems designed around **comparison, performance, and visibility**. They reward affirmation, emotional reaction, and constant engagement. For adults with a largely formed identity, this can already be destabilizing. For children and adolescents, it can be formative in deeply unhealthy ways.

Adolescence is a critical season of identity formation. Children are learning who they are, where they belong, and how they are perceived. Social media accelerates this process unnaturally. It **externalizes identity**, placing worth and belonging in metrics like likes, views, comments, and streaks. It trains children to monitor themselves constantly—how they look, how they sound, how they are received.

Comparison becomes unavoidable. Even seemingly harmless content invites measurement: bodies, friendships, humor, success, popularity. The conclusion is rarely generous. Someone always appears happier, more confident, more attractive, more desired.

What makes this especially concerning is how early this comparison begins. According to *The Digital Parenting Guidebook*, 49 percent of ten-to-twelve-year-olds are already using social media, despite nearly all major platforms requiring users to be at least thirteen years old.[32] This gap exists not because safeguards are robust, but because verification is minimal—often nothing more than entering a birth date or checking a box. In practice, access arrives years before children are developmentally prepared to interpret what they see.

This pressure is not abstract. Research reflects a visible downstream effect. In *The Opt-Out Family*, Erin Loechner cites data showing a sharp rise in cosmetic procedures driven by social-media appearance standards. One study reports that the number of plastic surgeons seeing patients motivated by looking better on social media has risen to 55 percent, with the fastest growth among patients under thirty—particularly teenagers.[33]

This is not merely about vanity; it reflects how early appearance-based identity is being internalized.

Social media also collapses context. Children encounter **adult conversations, adult humor, adult conflict, and adult sexuality** long before they have the cognitive or emotional tools to interpret them. Irony, outrage, and performative conflict dominate many platforms. Without guidance, these tones are absorbed as normal ways of relating.

Parents often underestimate this impact because social media feels familiar. But today's platforms operate at an unprecedented scale and speed. Algorithms are optimized for engagement—not development, not maturity, not well-being.

Research consistently shows a correlation between early social media use and increased anxiety, depression, and life dissatisfaction, particularly in early adolescence. Dr. Amy Orben of the University of Cambridge summarizes the cycle clearly: Social media use at certain life stages leads young people to be less satisfied with their lives—and when they are less satisfied, they turn to more social media.[34] This feedback loop is difficult even for adults to recognize. For children, it can become invisible.

Another cost is secrecy. Most children do not report troubling experiences on social media because they fear losing access. When belonging feels tied to a platform, disclosure feels risky. This leaves children carrying confusion, shame, or harm alone.

Delaying social media access is not about fear or denial. It is about timing. Identity formation requires space, stability, and relationships. Social media compresses and distorts that process. When social media is eventually introduced, it must come with transparency, conversation, and accountability. Shared passwords and parental review are not invasions of privacy; they are forms of guidance during formation.

I know a growing number of families who are choosing to delay social media access until the final year or two of high school, using it intentionally as a **transition to independence**, rather than a default milestone of childhood.

And yes—this includes Snapchat. Despite its framing as casual or "just a group thread," it carries significant risks related to FOMO, secrecy, and exposure. Its design actively discourages accountability and encourages impulsive communication.

Instagram Teens is also not a great compromise. While it may limit certain types of content, it does not address the deeper issue: a posture of distraction and constant evaluation. Children will have a lifetime to navigate social media. There is no developmental advantage to starting early—but there is measurable cost.

Children do not need social media to belong. They need relationship, presence, and time to grow without constant evaluation.

Summary: Why This Topic Matters

- Social media externalizes identity during a critical developmental window.
- Comparison and performance increase anxiety and dissatisfaction.
- Children encounter adult content without interpretive tools.
- Early access encourages secrecy and reduces disclosure.
- Delay protects formation; guidance supports independence.

#4 – Parental Controls

Why Tools Support Parenting but Never Replace It

Aside from moving to a farm and cutting off all technology, parental controls often feel like the most tangible response to technology anxiety. Filters, time limits, PIN codes, reports, and app restrictions promise order in a space that feels overwhelming. Used well, they help. Used alone, they disappoint.

The mistake many families make is not using parental controls; it is asking them to do more than they were designed to do.

Parental controls can restrict access, limit exposure, and increase visibility. They can block age-inappropriate streaming profiles, disable internet search on tablets, and monitor downloads on computers. They can slow things down and narrow the road. But they cannot form judgment. And they cannot replace relationships.

Even the best systems are porous. Research and parent reports consistently show that **a majority of children can find ways around security features**, whether through shared devices, alternate profiles, group chats, gaming audio, autoplay, ads, or platforms parents didn't know existed.

One widely cited study found that over 75 percent of surveyed youth reported being able to access online pornography at home without their caregiver knowing.[35] This is not a failure of vigilance; it is the nature of digital environments.

Another overlooked limitation is breakdown. Parental controls work differently across TVs, tablets, computers, and phones—and they work best when parents use native tools built into each operating system, rather than assuming one app can govern everything.

Even then, native controls are most reliable when children's digital access is already limited. Once open internet, YouTube, social media, or online gaming enter the picture, families often add third-party tools—gaining coverage, but not certainty.

This is why controls function best as guardrails, not walls. Guardrails narrow the road and slow speed, but they do not remove every hazard. Walls invite climbing. When restrictions feel absolute, invisible, or unexplained, children often respond with secrecy—learning how to bypass settings rather than how to discern wisely.

Over-restriction without conversation can also backfire. Children who fear losing access are far less likely to tell parents when something goes wrong. Silence becomes the safer option.

Parental controls are most effective when children know

- what is restricted,
- why it is restricted, and
- what to do if they encounter something concerning.

Controls should never be invisible. Transparency builds trust. When children understand that safeguards exist to protect their development—not to catch mistakes—they are more likely to cooperate and communicate.

One research finding underscores this clearly: Children are far more likely to seek help when they believe adults will respond calmly and supportively. Tools matter, but tone matters more.

Best Practices for Parental Controls Across Devices

The most effective parental control strategy begins with a simple principle: use the **native controls built into each device's operating system.**

On computers, parental controls are primarily designed to monitor internet use and manage app or program downloads, and they work best when parents rely on tools created for that specific platform.

- Microsoft Windows devices function most reliably with Microsoft Family Link and the Edge browser.
- Chromebooks with Google Family Link and Chrome browser.
- Apple laptops with Family Sharing and Screen Time paired with Safari browser.

While many third-party applications promise cross-platform coverage, in practice they are less consistent and often introduce gaps or conflicts. Alignment between hardware, operating system, and controls matters more than stacking tools.

Phones and tablets follow the same pattern, with an important distinction. Native parental controls—such as Google Family Link on Android devices and Screen Time within Apple Family Settings—are generally sufficient when children's access is intentionally limited. If social media, open internet browsing, online gaming, or streaming platforms are not permitted, native tools are often the most reliable, transparent, and cost-effective option.

However, once broader internet access is introduced, many families find it necessary to add third-party monitoring tools. Applications such as Bark,

Covenant Eyes, Qustodio, Aura, and others like Net Nanny or Norton Family can extend visibility across platforms, but they should be understood as supplemental, not comprehensive. Even the best tools require active parental engagement and clear expectations to be effective.

In practice, best outcomes come not from using more software, but from matching the level of technological freedom to the level of supervision and conversation a family can sustain. Parental controls work best when they are simple, platform-appropriate, and paired with ongoing dialogue—serving as guardrails that support healthy development rather than substitutes for parental presence.

I've heard it put this way in several places: We shouldn't hand our kids access to technology with immense potential for harm if we don't understand how to use the parental controls that come with it. Access without oversight isn't neutral; it's permission without protection. If a device requires guardrails for safe use, then knowing how to install and maintain those guardrails is part of responsible parenting.

Before we give freedom, we should understand the boundaries.

Summary: Why This Topic Matters

- Parental controls reduce exposure but cannot shape judgment.
- No system can block every harmful encounter.
- Over-reliance on controls can increase secrecy.
- Native tools work best within intentionally limited access.
- Controls are most effective when paired with explanation and trust.

#3 – Unstructured Play and the Non-Tech Environment

Why What Competes with Screens Determines Their Power

Screens rarely dominate a child's life in isolation. They dominate when nothing else competes effectively.

Children are drawn to technology because it is easy, stimulating, and rewarding. If the rest of a child's environment feels dull, demanding, or disconnected, screens will always win. This is why reducing screen time without enriching the surrounding environment often fails.

Unstructured play is not a luxury. It is a developmental necessity. When children are bored, something important is happening. Their imagination is activating. Their attention is learning to settle. Their bodies are learning how to rest without constant stimulation. These capacities develop only when space is left open.

Technology interrupts this process by design. Screens deliver instant engagement and remove the discomfort that boredom creates. Over time, children lose confidence in their ability to initiate play, sustain focus, or tolerate stillness. Boredom becomes something to escape rather than a doorway to creativity.

Parents often misinterpret boredom as a problem to solve. As a result, we let screens "occupy" them. In reality, boredom is a signal that internal resources are waking up. When screens immediately fill that space, children miss the chance to discover what they might create on their own.

A thoughtfully prepared environment changes everything. Homes that offer accessible alternatives—books, games, building materials, art supplies, outdoor space—make transitions away from screens far less contentious. These alternatives do not need to be elaborate. They need to be visible, usable, and affirmed.

Reducing screen time also requires increased parental presence. Children who are less occupied by screens will seek connection. They will ask questions. They will invite engagement. This is not a flaw in the plan; it is evidence that it is working.

I've heard several people put it this way: Boredom is not the enemy of childhood; it is the soil where creativity grows. This principle also explains why abrupt screen removal often backfires. When screens are taken away without strengthening the environment, children experience loss without replacement. When the environment is enriched first, limits feel less like deprivation and more like redirection.

Technology management is not primarily about subtraction. It is about cultivation. What children love will always reflect what their environment makes possible. When families invest in unstructured play and non tech rhythms, screens naturally lose some of their pull.

Summary: Why This Topic Matters

- Screens dominate when nothing meaningful competes with them.
- Unstructured play develops creativity, patience, and initiative.
- Boredom is a developmental gift, not a problem.
- A rich environment reduces resistance to screen limits.
- Reduced screen time requires increased parental presence.

#2 – Parents' Example and Attitudes

Why What Children See Shapes Them More Than What They Are Told

Before children understand rules, they understand patterns. Before they can articulate values, they absorb posture. This is why parental example matters more than any filter, rule, or technology plan.

Children do not primarily learn how to relate to technology through instruction. They learn through observation.

If screens regularly interrupt conversation, children learn that interruption is acceptable.

If phones consistently pull parents away, children learn that divided attention is expected.

If technology is treated with frustration or resentment, children learn that it is both irresistible and shameful.

Most of it happens unintentionally—through habits that feel reasonable in isolation.

Phones as Competition, Not Tools

One of the most sobering insights to emerge from classrooms and research is that children often experience phones not as neutral tools, but as competitors.

Research indicates that children report greater feelings of anger and sadness when parents frequently use smartphones during interactions, reflecting perceived reductions in attention and responsiveness.[36]

Children measure screen use relationally, not technically. They don't calculate necessity or duration. They feel when attention shifts. What they experience is not anger, but displacement. Rules alone cannot repair this. Only presence can.

Attitude Shapes the Emotional Climate

Equally formative is how parents talk about technology. Some parents are permissive and disengaged. Others are highly restrictive and resentful. Children feel both.

When parents regularly express irritation or contempt toward screens—especially while continuing to use them—children receive mixed signals.

Technology becomes something that is both desired and condemned. This tension often produces secrecy rather than wisdom.

There is a healthier posture, where we recognize technology is a good gift that requires boundaries. It is not feared. It is not worshiped. It is governed. This posture communicates stability. Children learn that limits are not reactions to panic, but expressions of care.

Modeling Self-Regulation

Perhaps the most important behavior parents can model is self-regulation.

Children need to see adults put phones down voluntarily. They need to watch parents choose presence over convenience. They need to hear adults name limits aloud: "I've been on this too long," or "I need to step away from this for a bit."

Summary: Why This Topic Matters

- Children learn how to relate to technology by watching their parents.
- Phones are often experienced as competitors for attention.
- Parental attitude shapes whether limits feel safe or hostile.
- Modeling self-regulation teaches discernment better than rules.
- Presence communicates value more powerfully than restriction.

#1 – Prevention and Ongoing Conversation

Why Relationship, Not Control, Is the Most Powerful Safeguard

If there is one topic that determines whether a family's technology efforts endure, it is this one.

No amount of restriction can fully protect a child in a digital world. No filter can anticipate every exposure. No plan can eliminate risk entirely.

This is not pessimism. It is reality. Because technology is woven into nearly every environment children inhabit, the most effective safeguard parents can offer is not tighter control, but intentional preparation rooted in relationship.

Prevention does not mean pretending danger does not exist. It means preparing children to recognize what they may encounter, understand it in age-appropriate ways, and know exactly what to do next—without fear.

From Avoidance to Readiness

One of the most important shifts parents must make is moving from avoidance to readiness. Children will encounter sexualized content, disturbing images, inappropriate language, and confusing interactions online. Stated simply, the question is not whether a child will encounter pornography—or other inappropriate material—but when that moment will come.

These encounters are far more often accidental than intentional, especially for younger children. They frequently arrive through innocent searches, autoplay recommendations, advertisements, group texts, gaming chats, or a friend's phone. Because these exposures are unexpected, they can be disorienting and difficult for children to process on their own.

Online gaming environments are a common example. Platforms like Roblox are often perceived as simple games, but in practice they function more like large online communities where players interact through chat and shared virtual spaces. While many of these interactions are harmless, the environment also makes it possible for children to encounter strangers—including adults—who attempt inappropriate conversations or manipulation. Most children are not seeking these interactions, but the structure of the platform makes them possible.

This is why preparation and ongoing conversation matter far more than assuming a platform designed for kids is automatically safe.

And this is where relationship matters most.

What the Research Shows About Silence and Non-Disclosure

In 2021, the nonprofit organization Thorn published a national study titled *Responding to Online Threats: Minors' Perspectives on Disclosing, Reporting, and Blocking.* Drawing on responses from more than two thousand children and teenagers ages nine to seventeen, the research examined not only what young people encounter online, but what they do—or do not do—after something harmful occurs.

One of the study's most sobering findings is how often children choose silence over sharing problems they encounter. Thorn reports that *one in four minors who experienced an online sexual interaction turned to no one for support.* [37] A significant number of children carry these experiences alone, without involving parents, caregivers, or trusted adults.

When asked why they stayed silent, most did not point first to fear or confusion—but to minimization. Nearly two-thirds said they chose not to report because they felt it was "not a big deal."[38] Many parents assume their child would speak up if something truly concerning happened—while research suggests the opposite.

Emotional barriers also play a powerful role. Thorn found that shame, embarrassment, fear of being misunderstood, and a desire to handle things independently all inhibit disclosure. For many children, silence is not passive. It is a calculated attempt to avoid judgment, escalation, or loss of autonomy with their tech. These are not fringe cases. They represent a consistent pattern across ages and platforms.

Perhaps most revealing is the gap between intention and behavior. While most children say they *would* report harmful experiences to an adult, far fewer actually do.[39] Good intentions dissolve quickly when embarrassment, fear of consequences, or uncertainty enters the picture. In fact, in another Thorn research, 1 in 3 minors who are survivors of "sextortion" never disclosed the experience.[40]

Taken together, the research reinforces a critical reality for parents: **Silence is common, secrecy is adaptive, and disclosure cannot be assumed.** Children are far more likely to manage harm privately—through blocking, ignoring, or minimizing—than to invite adult involvement. This is not a failure of character. It is a signal that trust, tone, and relational safety matter as much as rules and controls.

Creating an Open Invitation to Share

What shapes long-term outcomes is not whether exposure happens, but whether children know they can bring the experience into conversation.

Prepared children are far more resilient than sheltered but silent ones. When children don't speak up, the reasons are predictable:

- Fear of losing access
- Fear of disappointing parents
- Fear of punishment or overreaction
- Fear that adults won't understand

Rules without relational safety can unintentionally make children less safe. When honesty feels costly, silence feels protective.

Prevention works only when children believe—through experience—that telling the truth leads to help, not punishment. Parents must say it clearly and repeatedly: "If you see something confusing or upsetting, you will never be in trouble for telling us."

Simultaneously, "If you go looking for inappropriate content, we will limit your ability to use technology. But if you come across it unintentionally and tell us, opposed to us finding out other ways, you will not be in trouble." And then they must respond in ways that prove trust and integrity.

Preparing Without Creating Fear

One of the most effective tools for this kind of early preparation is the book *Good Pictures, Bad Pictures.*[41] Its strength is clarity, not alarm. It gives children language for what they may see, context for why it exists, and a simple response plan that reduces shame. Read together, it walks through real-life situations children will encounter and teaches them how to respond when they do.

Without a response plan, children often default to what many of us learned growing up: curiosity mixed with thrill, fear of consequences, some shame, and then silence. That combination is not healthy—and it is preventable.

Preparation like this does not make children anxious. It makes them less alone. When children already know what something is and what to do next, the experience loses much of its power.

I see this firsthand with my own teenager. He comes to me regularly when he hears, sees, or stumbles into inappropriate content—not because he is fearless, but because he knows telling me won't cost him access or trust if he wasn't seeking it out. We acknowledge what happened, thank him for telling us, adjust any safeguards if needed, and move on. That pattern has built confidence—for both of us.

The same principle applies to bullying, harassment, or predatory behavior. Prepared children are not immune to harm, but they are supported when it occurs.

Conversation as Ongoing Discipleship

Healthy conversation about technology is not reactive or interrogative. It is ongoing, curious, and relational. Parents who do this well ask questions not merely to correct behavior, but to understand experience:

- What do you enjoy about technology right now?
- When does it feel helpful—and when does it feel like too much?
- What kinds of things do kids your age run into online that feel uncomfortable?

These questions communicate safety. They tell children that technology is something the family navigates together.

Scripture consistently emphasizes formation of the heart, not just management of behavior. Digital parenting is a form of discipleship—helping children learn how to guard their hearts in a complex world.

If a child were learning a new sport, no parent would drop them off and disappear. The digital world deserves the same presence. Stay with them. Don't leave them alone in it.

Relationship Is the Real Safety Net

Filters will fail. Rules will be tested. Technology will continue to change faster than parents can keep up. But children who trust their parents will keep coming back—to ask questions, admit mistakes, and seek help.

Prevention is not a single talk. It is a culture built over years. And the strength of that culture depends far more on relationship than regulation.

When parents prioritize connection over control, children are far more likely to choose honesty over hiding—and wisdom over secrecy.

If you are curious to learn more, I have linked several books and other resources (particularly around having conversations) on my website for easy access.

Summary: Why This Topic Matters

- Exposure to harmful or confusing content is inevitable.
- Children's safety depends more on preparation than restriction alone.
- Fear silences; relational safety invites honesty.
- Thoughtful preparation reduces shame and secrecy.
- Ongoing conversation forms discernment, not dependence.

Looking Ahead to Making a Plan

The topics we've explored are not about eliminating risk, but about cultivating trust. We've seen that no filter can replace discernment, no restriction can surpass preparation, and no rule can substitute for relationship. What keeps children safe isn't the absence of exposure, but the presence of open, ongoing conversation. As we shift toward building your technology plan, remember that the foundation is relational safety. With that in place, your plan will be far more than rules; it will be a roadmap for raising wise, honest, and resilient kids in a digital world.

Chapter 9

The Technology Plan: A Livable Family Framework

In this chapter, we'll walk through the core variables that lead to a successful technology plan in the home.

A technology plan is meant to bring clarity and stability to daily life, not add strain or confusion. It doesn't need to be complex, but it does need to be intentional. Taking time on the front end to think through expectations, limits, and follow-through prevents misunderstandings and unnecessary conflict later. The initial effort is what allows the plan to function smoothly once it's in place.

At a high level, a successful technology plan rests on five primary components:

1. Work through the template (available for free at www.RichRoadStewardship.com).
2. Prepare and hold a formal family meeting.
3. Post the plan publicly so expectations remain visible.
4. Parents model the behavior they are asking of their children.
5. Parents remain available and engaged as the plan is lived out.

That's it. This is the basic structure of a healthy technology plan and its rollout.

This chapter explores these elements in more depth, but my hope is that your experience implementing them feels clear and manageable. There are certainly nuances—every family has them—but these five practices do the heavy lifting.

When a plan becomes too complicated or overly subjective, it tends to break down. Parents grow tired, kids disengage, and consistency erodes. Simplicity, clarity, and follow-through are what carry the day.

Technology Plans: Where the Rubber Meets the Road

Most families don't struggle with technology because they don't care. They struggle because they never made a plan. In nearly every seminar I teach, I ask the room a simple question before we begin: "How many of you have a written or intentional technology plan for your home?"

Roughly 90 percent of the hands stay down.

If that's you, you're not behind—you're normal. But we are now living in a moment where "winging it" is no longer a neutral option. Technology creep is real, and it has quietly woven itself into the fabric of family life.

Technology rarely storms into a home all at once. It drifts in. A show here. A tablet there. A phone "just for safety." A laptop "just for school." And then one day, parents realize they are negotiating constantly, reacting emotionally, and arguing about screens far more than they ever intended. At that point, technology is no longer a tool. It is setting the agenda.

A technology plan is simply the decision—made *in advance* and communicated clearly—about what children are allowed to do with technology, for how long, and under what conditions. A good plan gives parents shared language, reduces daily conflict, and provides children with consistent expectations. Most importantly, it allows technology to be managed *before* it becomes relationally corrosive.

As you've already seen throughout this book, privilege without responsibility breeds entitlement. Technology is one of the greatest privileges modern children receive—and without a plan, it becomes one of the fastest accelerators of entitlement in the home.

Technology Is Not a Single Thing

One of the most common mistakes families make is treating "technology" as a single category.

Think back to your own childhood. Most of us grew up with limited and contained technology: a television with a handful of channels, a VCR and a CD or DVD player, a radio/boombox, maybe a gaming system, and eventually a slow family computer with dial-up internet. Phones were tethered to walls and cordless phones had limited range (depending on the length of their antenna). Even the microwave once felt revolutionary.

Today, technology is fundamentally different. It is networked, personalized, persuasive, and endless. It is designed to learn us, keep us engaged, and connect us—constantly—to content, people, and products.

Instead of a television with ten channels and a shelf of movies, we now have streaming platforms with thousands of options. Instead of limited media, we have infinite media. Instead of hard stops, we have endless and curated feeds for media.

Consider the reach of today's technology categories—and where, if anywhere, their limits actually end:

- Television and streaming
- YouTube
- Tablets
- Video games
- Smartphones
- Computers
- Social media
- Messaging platforms

Each category impacts children differently. Each carries different risks. Each requires different boundaries and tools. A plan that treats all technology the same will always feel arbitrary and confusing. Good plans are specific.

The Purpose of a Technology Plan

A well-designed technology plan serves two primary purposes:

1. **Protection during formation**. Children's brains, emotional regulation, and identity are still developing. A plan limits exposure and overuse during a vulnerable season of life.

2. **Digital discipleship**. Technology becomes a training ground for self-control, honesty, responsibility, and wisdom—not just something to endure until adulthood.

This is why your plan should be written down, posted publicly, and revisited regularly. Families who keep their plan "in their head" inevitably drift back into negotiation and inconsistency. Don't ask me how I know that.

The Four Questions Every Technology Plan Must Answer

Across every seminar and resource I've seen, one framework appears again and again—because it works. Every technology plan must clearly answer four questions:

1. Which devices can be used?
2. Who can use them?
3. When can they be used?
4. Where can they be used?

Posting these answers somewhere visible removes daily debate. Parents stop being the referee. The plan becomes the authority.

Conviction Comes Before Enforcement

Technology plans are easy to write and hard to hold—unless parents know *why* they're doing it.

For me, unmanaged technology began to feel like a wedge in my relationship with my kids. It was always present, always competing for attention. I found myself reactive, impatient, and subtly resentful—both of the technology and of the tension it created. And entitlement was growing in the gap between privilege and responsibility.

My "why" was relationship.

I realized that a clear, communicated plan could preserve future relationship by helping us now. When I understood that a technology plan—like a chores plan—was to my kids' advantage (and mine), I had what I needed to hold the line.

That conviction matters. Without conviction, parents fold under pressure with complex dynamics like technology. At its core, a Technology Plan should be rooted in a simple, shared belief: *We want to raise grateful, grounded kids who understand how life works and know they are deeply loved. We don't want technology to create a barrier in our relationship with our kids.*

Everything else flows from that.

A Plan Is Not a Prison

Many parents worry that a technology plan will feel rigid or joyless. In practice, the opposite is true.

Families with clear plans consistently report

- less arguing
- less nagging

- fewer emotional blow-ups
- more enjoyment of screen time when it's allowed
- more peace when it's not

A plan allows celebration without guilt. Screen days or screen times become something kids anticipate rather than demand. Boredom is no longer a crisis; it's expected.

And importantly, exceptions become easier. Generosity only works when there is a baseline to be generous from.

Core Principles That Make a Technology Plan Work

A technology plan does not rise or fall on the number of rules it contai

In previous chapters, I outlined the core topics and principles—ordered from least to most important—that guide healthy technology management in the home. Those same principles are at work here. The goal was first to clarify *what we are solving for*, so that now we can make concrete decisions, define boundaries, and write them down.

Before moving forward, I encourage you to download the technology plan templates for families, teens, and younger children from my website, or use the workbook if you have it. Having something in front of you will make this process far more practical.

Depending on the format available on the website at the time you download it (I'll continue improving this over time), you may receive it as a stand-alone PDF. If so, you can download the file, upload it to Google Docs, and customize it however you'd like.

For now, we'll focus on building a technology plan for the family. I am walking through this next section in the order of the current Technology Plan Template for Family's on my website.

#1 – Family Vision for Technology

After years of trying to manage technology in our home tactically, I eventually realized part of the problem was that I lacked a clear vision for it. I was focused on rules and controls without first asking what I actually wanted technology to *do*—or not do—in our family. I never would have guessed how helpful simply clarifying that vision would be.

Ours is pretty simple: "Technology is a powerful gift that can be used for learning, creativity, connection, and service. It is a tool and not a treasure. As a Christian family, we commit to steward technology in a way that honors God, strengthens relationships, protects hearts and minds, and supports our calling to love God and love others (see Matthew 22:37–39)."

There it is. Technology is powerful (potential), it is a gift (it's not bad) and it can be productive. Technology is a tool, not a treasure, and something we will use to honor God, our family, and others.

We're calling it out with our kids. Technology isn't just something out there, it is something powerful that can be used for great good or great harm. And like anything else with great potential, it comes responsibility. We like the 1 Corinthians 6:12 passage, highlighting that just because we "can" doesn't mean we "should."

#2 – Core Principles

This is something that we cover together and assume our kids will forget, but we can return to it later when needed.

Technology should be productive if we are stewarding it well and should prioritize certain things:

- Serve people and not replace relationships.
- Support spiritual growth, not crowd it out.
- Protect purity, dignity, and mental health.
- Encourage responsibility, honesty, and self-control.
- Be age appropriate.

And you may notice that not all of these things fit perfectly in there—but it's a good place to put the principles for future conversation. If our kids are out of control with technology, and wearing thin because of drama in group-text threads or otherwise, we can bring them back here and let them know that's not surprising, and we need to take a break.

#3 – Devices Allowed in Our Home

See the template, check the boxes. Again, this may seem obvious, but now we're naming it. You (the parent) are the IT department, remember? This is your inventory of equipment available for use in the home. It's not a free world when kids are in your home.

And it identifies ownership. As you will see, I put two boxes for optional checking: "family-owned" and "child-owned." Most people will likely click "family-owned" or "parent-owned," which just tells the kids that when things feel out of control, they don't own the device they have privileges to use.

Just as easily as privileges were given, if they become a nuisance, obstruction, or a life-suck, they can be paused or taken away.

#4 – Who Can Use What

This is a big one. Not all devices can be used by all people. Our younger kids struggle to understand why their older siblings get more access to things than they do. That's normal. We have our ways of explaining.

More importantly, have you taken time to list out who can use what and under what conditions?

It may feel like you're putting it in their face if they have half as much access as their older siblings—but it's also the reality. They also probably have half as many chores. If it's the reality, then state it as fact, and let them know if they continue to be respectful and teachable with what they have, they, too, will have increased access and devices in due time.

#5 – When Technology May Be Used

I love this one. Relying on "oral tradition" to manage this can really become riddled with conflicting memory. I put boxes you can check (or add to) on your plan as you build it, or you can leave boxes unchecked.

You can see Permitted Times and Technology-Free Times.

What I like most about this is it allows you to have ground rules from which you can make exceptions. We like to avoid technology being out during meals, family gatherings, right before bedtime (we fudge on that one more than others), mornings before school (absolutely no TV before school in our home), on Sundays, and during times of worship, prayer, or devotions.

For permitted times, we can be more specific when we get to #9 on screen time.

#6 – Where Technology May Be Used

See sheet, although we say it out loud. We do not allow any technology in the bedrooms, bathrooms, or behind closed doors.

This one is pretty straightforward for us.

#7 – Content Standards

This one can be a little more difficult to manage with just parental controls, so we spell it out. We request that any content we are watching is appropriate (see the template for examples).

Do we abide by this perfectly? No. Is it a little restrictive? Yes. Do I have a better plan for now? Not really. Is that okay? Yup, I'm trying, and I'm learning, and adapting as needed.

It really gives us, again, the ability to say, "The content you watch, video games you play, things you look up on the internet, have to be age appropriate."

And this is where we let our kids know that we have parental controls on and can review what is seen and not seen at our discretion. In some cases we'll get weekly reports that show what things have been flagged so we can review them with the kids.

This is so healthy for the kids to know. They need to know Mom and Dad aren't in the dark. They appreciate knowing that we can see everything (even if we can't always) and that prevents them from unnecessary temptation.

#8 – Social Media, Messaging, and Online Interactions

We identify at what age social media accounts are available. We're doing senior year of high school for now.

We use this section to make sure our kids know they need to be kind when functioning online, to not share anything they would be embarrassed for the world to see or that they would not say face-to-face with a person in public, and to never share personal information.

Again, this is a document for us to return to when needed. They will make mistakes, and these are the guidelines for operating.

#9 – Screen Time and Balance

We eventually chose to use "screen days" instead of daily hour limits. We tried tracking minutes and time windows, but with four kids it became nearly impossible to manage. Somehow, no one ever used all their screen time for the day. Everyone always seemed to have "just twenty more minutes" left.

For us, we identified "screen days." Tuesday, Thursday, Saturday. On those days, they get two to three hours (and we may allow more), but only on those days. There are exceptions, of course, but generally speaking that's the deal.

On this template, you can identify what days and hours are available for screens.

Again, for us, simpler was better. Our kids do not balk on non-screen days. They wake up knowing they aren't going to have access to TV or video games at home on those days, and I really think as a result they just move on to the other things available to them.

It's much easier for us to manage, as well.

#10 – Accountability and Review

Here we are stating that parents are allowed to review device use and content at will, and that we can and will talk openly about limits, content, temptations, mistakes, and adjustments to the plan.

We identify how often the plan may be reviewed, so that kids know intrinsically this is fluid and not concrete. That's in their favor, actually, because if they are growing in maturity and readiness, it may mean some additional liberty or privilege can be added.

#11 – Grace, Growth, and Redemption

In this short section, we're taking some time to make sure our kids hear us say out loud (if we haven't already) that mistakes are going to happen, and that when they do, we expect honesty and will respond with grace and guidance. It tells the kids that this stuff can be complicating and temptations abound. When they do, we need to be able to know how to work through it together, and for them to know that we aren't going to come down on them like a hammer.

#12 – Family Commitment

This step is your opportunity to make sure everyone understands that the technology plan has been read, discussed, and agreed upon. In many ways, it's simply a formality—but an important one.

Surprisingly often, our kids will insist, "You never told us that. I swear you didn't. I know you didn't." It can make you feel a little crazy—until you walk over together to the fridge, point to the technology plan posted there, and calmly read the document that includes their signatures confirming that everything was discussed and that nothing has changed since.

Clarity has a way of lowering the temperature in the room. It deescalates the situation quickly— it's more for them than you—but just as much for you as them . . . well, you know what I'm saying. Clarity is confidence and avoids unnecessary conflict.

You may wish to add your own sections to the plan:

- Technology Guidelines During Sleepovers
- What Is Allowed When Friends Are at Our House
- Clear Consequences (Probably Technology!)

Other Final Thoughts on Succeeding with Technology Plans

Technology Plans Create Space for Boredom

Technology short-circuits boredom by design. Infinite feeds, autoplay, and fast-paced imagery push children past boredom into overstimulation—and then into anxiety. This is why good technology plans intentionally preserve boredom. They create spaces where nothing is happening and something must be invented. Children may resist this at first. That resistance is not a sign of failure—it is a sign that the plan is working.

Parents' Attitudes Shape the Culture

No technology plan survives if parents resent it.

Children are highly attuned to tone. When parents are constantly irritated by screens, kids feel judged. When parents model healthy habits and a calm posture, boundaries feel safer.

Parents' example remains the single most powerful influence on children's technology habits.

Presence Is the Real Substitute

Reducing screen time always requires one thing: **more of us**. Screens often function as a substitute for connection, not because children prefer devices to parents, but because devices are predictable and parents are busy. When screens go away, children will seek what they actually want—time, attention, and presence.

This is why technology plans should never be separated from the larger vision of family life. The goal is not less technology; it is more relationship.

Having a game plan for how you are going to fill the time you have recaptured from screens is important to think about in advance of rolling out a technology plan. Maybe add a game night, or a movie night, or an activity night to the schedule. They'll love that—maybe not at first, but they'll see soon enough.

Also, unlike how we rolled out the chores plan (started immediately), we left a few days in between when our technology plan was rolled out and when it went into effect. We prepared them for the change, and counted down the days, and when it came, it was what it was.

We rolled it out on a screen day—and let them have a good bit of screens that day.

And then we were ready. The kids thought some of our initial efforts to fill the space and time were shallow (same ideas I shared above), but that's because they were comparing those family activities to stimulating screen time.

Within days, the kids were actually enjoying our new format. Did they ask for screens still? Sure. But they weren't demanding about it.

Consequences Must Be Predictable

Technology consequences should not be emotional or dramatic. They should be predictable and relationally calm.

When consequences feel reactive, kids focus on the punishment.

When consequences feel inevitable, kids focus on their choices.

Effective plans include

- clear consequences for dishonesty
- clear consequences for bypassing controls
- temporary loss of privileges—not permanent bans
- restoration pathways (what earns access back)

If you get fired up when rules are broken or your kids dismiss your requests, it's really helpful to take a breath. Taking some time to cool down before enforcing a consequence protects both authority and relationship.

Anger teaches fear. Consistency teaches wisdom.

The Super-Important Family Meeting

Just as with chores and work, how you *introduce* the technology plan matters as much as what it contains.

I have a recommended rollout that is intentionally ceremonial:

- Choose a calm, unrushed time.
- Have food or dessert.
- Explain the *why* before the rules.

- Invite questions.
- Acknowledge what will be hard.
- Consider starting soon, but not immediately.

This communicates respect and seriousness.

We leave lots of time for questions and discussion. We let them know we are open to adapting things, but not likely to just concede.

We explain we are working to give them more time separated from screens because of their need for healthy mental development. We explain (to our kids who are 8+ years old) that screen time is fun but functions like sugar: too much sugar makes the body sick. Too much screen time makes your brain sick.

In moderation, screen time is great and to be enjoyed. At least that's what I think.

Exceptions Will Happen—But Keep Them Exceptional

Healthy plans allow exceptions, but they name them explicitly.

Exceptions work when

- they are clearly framed as exceptions
- they are tied to celebration or circumstance
- they do not replace the norm

When exceptions become frequent, the plan erodes.

Children are surprisingly resilient with firm boundaries when those boundaries are fair, predictable, and relationally grounded.

What Success Actually Looks Like

Success does not mean zero conflict. It does not mean perfect compliance. It does not mean kids who never want screens.

Success looks like

- less secrecy
- fewer arguments
- more unstructured play
- more conversation
- more peace
- stronger relationships

Over time, children raised within clear technology boundaries develop something far more valuable than self-control alone: discernment.

They learn when to engage and when to step away. They learn that not every desire must be satisfied. They learn that life is bigger than a screen.

A Final Word on Technology

Technology is not going away. The goal of a technology plan is not to win a war against screens. It is to shepherd hearts, protect formation, and preserve relationship in a confusing age.

Just as with money and work, structure creates freedom. And freedom, over time, creates gratitude and grounding. That is stewardship.

Big Idea

A technology plan turns conviction into a livable family framework. Technology will always set the agenda unless parents decide—clearly, ahead of time—how it will function in the home. A written, shared plan protects formation, reduces conflict, and allows technology to serve family life rather than compete with it.

20 Key Takeaways

1. Most families struggle with technology not because they don't care, but because they never made a plan.
2. Winging it is no longer neutral. Technology creep fills any space left undefined.
3. Technology is not one thing.
4. TVs, tablets, phones, computers, games, and social platforms affect children differently and require different boundaries. Good plans are specific.
5. A technology plan protects formation and discipleship.
6. It limits exposure during vulnerable developmental years and trains wisdom, self-control, and discernment.
7. Conviction must come before enforcement.
8. Parents need a clear "why" or they will fold under pressure. Relationship—not control—is the goal.
9. Clarity lowers conflict.
10. When expectations are written, posted, and agreed upon, parents stop being referees and kids stop negotiating.
11. Plans create freedom, not restriction.

12. Families with clear plans report less arguing, more enjoyment when screens are allowed, and more peace when they are not.
13. Modeling matters more than rules.
14. What parents practice around attention teaches louder than what they mandate.
15. Boredom is a feature, not a bug.
16. Good plans intentionally preserve boredom because it fuels creativity, resilience, and imagination.
17. Consequences must be predictable and calm.
18. Consistency teaches wisdom; anger teaches fear.
19. Technology plans succeed when they are relational, flexible, and revisited over time.
20. Growth can lead to greater trust and expanded privilege.

The Technology Plan – The Basics

1. Clarify the family vision for technology (tool, not treasure).
2. Define core principles that guide decisions.
3. List devices allowed and ownership (family-owned vs. child-owned).
4. Specify who can use what.
5. Define when technology may be used (and when it may not).
6. Define where technology may be used (shared spaces only, etc.).
7. Set content standards and accountability expectations.
8. Address social media, messaging, and online interactions.
9. Decide on screen-time structure (e.g., screen days vs. daily limits).
10. Name accountability and review rhythms.
11. State grace and restoration pathways.
12. Hold a family meeting and sign the plan.

Chapter 10

Chores, Privileges, and Creating a Plan

If you'd like to follow along more actively as you begin this chapter, you may find it helpful to download the **Chores Planning Document** at www.RichRoadStewardship.com under the **Resources** tab and use it as a template while you read.

Chores, Shared Ownership, and the Role of Privileges

If childhood is practice for adulthood, then chores are one of the most overlooked practice fields we have. Most parents know this instinctively. We want our kids to help around the house. We want them to learn responsibility. We want them to pitch in without constant reminders or complaining. And yet, for many families, chores feel far more complicated than they should.

They turn into power struggles.

They trigger frustration.

They feel personal.

Parents nag. Kids resist. Everyone gets tired. And eventually, many families quietly give up or settle for far less than they know is healthy.

This chapter exists to say a few things clearly. First, chores are not about keeping a clean house—although the house will get cleaned. Second, winning with chores is not about finding the perfect system—although a good system goes a long way, as we'll see.

Rather, chores are about inviting our kids into caring for our environment and teaching them how life works. And when chores and work are framed and handled that way, they stop being a relational drain and start becoming a stabilizing force in a home.

Why Chores Matter More Than We Think

Work in the home provides children something almost nothing else can: a lived sense of belonging.

As our family grew, we became exposed to Montessori education—initially out of curiosity, not conviction. What drew us in was not a trend or technique, but a view of childhood that was both demanding and developmental. Montessori begins with a challenging assumption: Children are capable of far more than we often believe.

Growth, in this framework, happens through real engagement with their surrounding environment. When adults step in too quickly—fixing, rescuing, smoothing—we often interrupt the very development we hope to encourage.

Montessori's conclusions were not theoretical. They emerged from decades of careful observation of children in real environments. Her central insight was developmental: Children possess an internal drive toward independence, and healthy adults are formed when that drive is respected, guided, and gradually entrusted with real responsibility.

Her well-known phrase—"Help me do it myself"—captures this vision. Independence does not grow because adults step aside completely, nor because children are forced into performance. It grows when adults prepare environments that invite participation, responsibility, and increasing competence.

Freedom, in this view, is never detached from structure. Children are given meaningful choices within clear limits. Expectations are calm and consistent. The goal is not efficiency, but mastery—learning how to act competently in the world.

Children trusted with real responsibility develop a quiet sense of capability. They learn that effort matters, that mistakes are part of learning, and that growth requires engagement rather than avoidance. That same principle applies at home.

Chores are not primarily about obedience or cleanliness—though both may result. They are about life. Shared work and mutual care of a space are how families function. To withhold meaningful work from children is not kindness; it is a subtle form of handicap. Chores teach effort, service, follow-through, and belonging—being part of something larger than oneself.

Children, of course, develop unevenly. Young children are naturally self-focused. Empathy and the ability to see a different perspective unfold gradually, often between ages seven and twelve, and adolescence introduces its own season of insecurity and resistance. As a result, children respond to responsibility differently. Compliance may mask anxiety; resistance may reflect development rather than defiance.

We rarely see the full story behind behavior. This is why guided chores matter for every child. For the compliant child, chores teach that love is not earned through performance, even though their contribution is genuinely needed. For the resistant child, chores communicate belonging: You matter here because you are part of this family. We need your help, and are going to hold you accountable.

When responsibility is introduced with patience, clarity, and grace, the outcome for both is the same: belonging.

The Real Reason Chores Break Down

If chores are so important, why do they go so badly in so many homes?

From teaching and trial-and-error in my own family, I've found that chores usually fail for a small handful of reasons—and they all tend to reinforce one another.

- Parents are busy and short on margin.
- Expectations are unclear or inconsistent.
- Accountability is informal or dependent on reminders.
- Consequences are vague, emotional, or unenforced.
- Parents grow frustrated and disengage.

When this happens, kids don't become more responsible — they become confused. And confusion breeds resistance.

Most kids are not refusing chores because they are malicious or lazy. They are responding to an environment where the expectations change, the follow-through is inconsistent, and the emotional tone feels unpredictable.

That's not a discipline problem. It's a systems problem. And systems can be rebuilt.

Shared Ownership Changes Everything

One of the most important shifts parents can make is moving from "getting help around the house" to "shared ownership of the home." Those are not the same thing. Again, we're dealing with little people brains and hearts, which are rapidly changing and forming every week.

When chores are framed as helping Mom or Dad, kids often feel like assistants who can opt out. When chores are framed as shared ownership, kids will begin to understand that the home belongs to everyone, and everyone contributes.

In our family, this shift **was** the turning point. Because it answered the one major question that has ruled children since the dawn of time: "Why?" *Why, you ask? Because we need your help.*

We stopped asking our kids to help "us" as parents and started telling them—calmly and clearly—that we needed them. This home exists for our family, and caring for it together is part of being in the family. That language matters.

When children understand that their work is necessary, not optional, something changes. They stop negotiating as much. They stop feeling singled out. And over time, they begin to take pride in their role.

Today, our kids handle roughly 80 percent of the weekly household workload. That doesn't mean perfection. It doesn't mean deep cleaning everything. But it does mean the house runs better because they are involved—and remarkably, it runs with far less conflict than before.

Baseline Chores vs. Paid Work

One of the most common questions parents ask is whether kids should be paid for chores.

There are several approaches that can work. But the key distinction I've found helpful for us is this: Some work is required because you are part of the family. Some work can earn money because it goes beyond that baseline.

For us, baseline chores are not paid. They are the cost of membership in the household. Things like dishes, laundry, trash, bathrooms, living rooms, play areas, floors, pet care, and general upkeep fall into this category for us. These are expected, and they are tied to privileges, not pay.

Paid work comes later, and it is optional. Larger projects. Yard work. One-time cleaning jobs. Babysitting. Washing cars. Organizational tasks. These are opportunities to earn money, especially when kids are too young to work outside the home.

This blended approach works well because it teaches two important truths at the same time:

- Life requires contribution even when no one is paying you.
- When you want something beyond the basics, work creates opportunity to earn money.

That distinction helps kids avoid entitlement while building agency.

Accountability Without Nagging

The biggest breakthrough for many families is not simply making a chores chart—it's building accountability that doesn't depend on constant reminders or chore charts that fail to get updated (that was me).

Any system can work if it does one thing well: It makes expectations visible and allows kids to track their own completion without creating confusion.

This can be a whiteboard, a chore chart, a clipboard, a digital tablet, or a tool like Skylight. The format matters far less than the principle. But honestly, Skylight has been a gamechanger for us. More on that in a minute.

Kids should be able to

- see what is expected for the day;
- mark tasks complete themselves; and
- know when something is missed without being told repeatedly.

Parents should verify completion calmly, not chase it emotionally.

When accountability is externalized into a system, parents stop being the reminder, the enforcer, and the bad guy. The system does the teaching. And, as we'll see, consequences enforce good habits.

Skylight – A Tool That Actually Helps

Most parents don't fail at chores because they lack conviction. They fail because the system requires too much energy to maintain.

Whiteboards and paper charts work well for many (most) families—I've used them. But when they aren't updated consistently, or kids misinterpret what day of the week it is, sometimes reminders pile up, expectations blur, and parents become the system, the enforcer, and the bad guy. We, as parents, were not great at keeping them updated.

One of the most helpful tools we've used is the digital Skylight calendar (which includes a chores chart function). Not because it's flashy, but because it quietly removes some of that friction. It sits on our kitchen counter, the screen is on all day serving two primary functions—chores, and access to a family calendar.

I know many families are working hard to reduce technology's footprint in their home; we are there with you. However, this is one of those, in my opinion, exceptionally good digital tools that highlights the virtue of digital benefits in our day without overcomplicating things.

First, it refreshes automatically each morning from a pre-scheduled list of daily tasks for each child. We don't have to rewrite or reset anything. It simply shows what matters today. That daily clarity is powerful. Kids don't see a long, overwhelming list or matrix—they see what's due now, today. The task feels manageable, which lowers resistance.

Second, completion is visible. Chores can be checked off easily. Kids get closure. Parents can see progress at a glance without nagging. The system becomes the reminder, not the parent.

Third, as an added bonus, it integrates activity calendars and family calendars. Kids see practices, school events, and upcoming family events for that day or into the future if they want to see what's happening that day, that week, or that month.

There are less expensive alternatives, and some families do fine with them. That said, I've watched several families try to save money with knock-off versions, only to end up switching to Skylight later. That doesn't mean there aren't other solid options—but in our experience, the reliability and simplicity have made it worth it.

Privileges: The Magic That Makes Chores Matter

One of the reasons chore systems fail is not because parents assign the wrong tasks or choose the wrong tools. They fail because chores are disconnected from anything that feels real to kids.

When chores exist in isolation, free from real consequences—when they are assigned, ignored, nagged about, and eventually done out of exhaustion—they lose their formative power. They become noise. Kids don't feel their weight. Parents don't feel their effectiveness. Everyone disengages.

Privileges change that. Privileges give chores substance. Privileges elevate responsibility from "something parents want" to "something kids care about." They take chores out of the abstract and anchor them in daily life in a way children immediately understand.

Privileges are not entitlements.

They are not rights.

They are extra, and fun, and special.

And because of that, they are powerful teachers. We all love our privileges!

In our home, privileges include things like screen time, video games, playing with friends, sports and activities, jumping on the trampoline, use of a smartphone (our teenager), having a dog, staying up late on Friday nights to watch a movie together as a family, and other freedoms that are enjoyable but not essential. These are not basic needs. They are benefits. And benefits are maintained by responsibility.

When chores are done, privileges are kept. When chores are not done, privileges are lost. That's it.

No lectures. No bargaining. No emotional escalation. Privileges become something to *keep*, and something that can be *lost*. That reality alone gives chores meaning.

There are other streams of thought that encourage parents to not do allowances, and rather payout for every chore—thus teaching kids that if you want something, you work for it and earn the money. This approach is hyper-focused on teaching kids the work/reward relationship. Honestly, a very worthy goal!

We did this for a while years ago, and in my experience (which is limited in that regard) I found it frustrating, because a child could then sort of choose not to work. Especially around seasons of birthdays or holidays where gifts abound, they become useless (they wait for the money to flow in!).

At the same time, we found ourselves wondering, *Are these chores actually optional?*

Chores and Money – A Clarification

As Beth Kobliner, author of *Make Your Kid a Money Genius (Before Graduating High School)*, points out, there's a common but important distinction to be made between chore systems that build character and chore-for-pay systems that inadvertently create transactional thinking:

> Research shows that chores are good for kids because they teach responsibility and the importance of chipping in to help others. But it's a mistake to link those chores to money. Unless you're

> willing to negotiate each time you want your kid to empty the dishwasher or put his clothes in the hamper, steer clear of systems that pay per chore.[42]

Kobliner's point aligns with a deeper formation principle: Contribution within the family is first about belonging and responsibility, not earning or bargaining. When chores become a menu of optional tasks tied to cash rewards, children can learn the *wrong lesson*—that contribution is something you do only when compensated.

In other words, chores should help children see themselves as *contributors*, not *contractors.*

Finally, even if we started that up again, we still have the whole topic of privileges in play. We found (this is just us) that it was more plain and helpful to attach privileges to chores, and then have some extra work (we call jobs) that they can earn money for.

It turns out, privileges are powerful.

Why Privileges Must Be Both Kept and Lost

For privileges to work, they must function in both directions.

If privileges are only ever given and rarely taken away, they become entitlements.

If privileges are taken unpredictably or emotionally, they become punishments.

Neither of those forms children well. Privileges must be

- clearly defined;
- consistently tied to responsibility;
- calmly enforced; and
- predictable in outcome.

When kids know what privileges they have, what responsibilities maintain them, and what happens when responsibilities are missed, the system becomes self-teaching.

The privilege does the talking. This is where many parents hesitate. We worry that removing privileges will damage the relationship or feel too harsh. But when privileges are framed correctly, their removal doesn't feel personal—it feels logical.

The message is not, "I'm mad at you." The message is, "This is how life works." That distinction matters enormously. Kids may be disappointed.

They may be frustrated. But they are rarely confused. And confusion, more than disappointment, is what fuels resentment.

And to be sure, there are plenty of privileges that are off-limits. If we have a movie night scheduled for the family on Friday with popcorn and pop, that's not on the table to be taken away. Their sports events are rarely something to lose—unless there's a real lesson to teach in context to them.

Sometimes parents struggle not because they lack consequences, but because they lack meaningful privileges to remove. That can be a signal—not of failure but of opportunity.

In some homes, it may actually be wise to introduce a few additional privileges (stay with me here) with the clear understanding that privileges are earned, maintained, and, when necessary, removed. This isn't manipulation; it's about creating leverage that genuinely matters to your children.

We live in a culture saturated with privilege. Our kids see it every day—in their friends' homes, on their teams, in the stores we visit, and online. Whether we welcome it or resist it, they are constantly comparing. What shapes them is not only what we provide or withhold, but how they perceive their environment.

Some parents intentionally pull back on certain privileges to avoid overstimulation or entitlement, and that instinct is understandable. We're there with you. But if a child's environment feels dull to them, and they are simultaneously resistant to chores and responsibility, that may be worth exploring. I won't prescribe what that looks like for your family. But sometimes adding a little "fun spice" to the home—paired with clear expectations and consequences—creates an environment that feels more engaging and relational, not less.

The goal is not to make life harsher, but more formative. Privileges teach when they matter in the eyes of the one with the privilege. And when parents struggle to find consequences with any real "bite," thoughtfully adding a few meaningful privileges can create motivation with far less conflict than constant correction.

Privileges Teach Reality Better Than Lectures Ever Will

Privileges are one of the most effective ways to teach children about cause and effect.

In adult life, privileges function in a similar way, though with greater complexity. If we want to take fun trips as a family, we need to show up to work and do our jobs well. When we perform faithfully, we may earn raises, added opportunities, or greater flexibility—benefits that allow us to bless others or enjoy new experiences. If we neglect our work or choose not to work at all, income will likely decline, opportunities will shrink, and many of those privileges naturally disappear.

In summary, we keep privileges and freedoms by handling responsibility well. When we connect chores to privileges, we are not being harsh. We are rehearsing adulthood in small, manageable ways.

Kids learn that

- effort matters;
- consistency matters;
- responsibility precedes freedom; and
- choices have outcomes.

Those lessons don't require speeches. They require systems. Privileges are the system. It speaks for itself. We say less, they learn more.

Becoming a Great Manager

This brings us to an important shift in how we think about parenting. One of the most helpful reframes I've adopted when it comes to chores and work in the home—and often share in presentations—is this: You are your child's first manager.

That can sound uncomfortable. No parent wants to run their home like a corporation or treat their children like employees. Marcus Buckingham famously observed, "People leave managers, not companies."[43]

In the workplace, the environment a leader creates deeply shapes whether people thrive or disengage, whether they show up enthusiastically or do just enough to find other opportunities.

At home, the dynamic is even more consequential. Our children don't get to choose their "manager." For years, we are the primary authority shaping the environment in which they learn to work, contribute, and grow.

That reality carries weight. Most children won't "quit" their parents, but they often disengage and do the minimum required. Being a great manager at home doesn't mean being rigid or demanding. In fact, the best leaders are thoughtful, consistent, and calm. They communicate expectations clearly. They follow through. They correct without humiliation. They lead with steadiness.

For better or worse, our children will one day look back on their childhood as a reference point for how they hope to lead their own families—and that's healthy. Increasingly, that realization motivates me toward patience and consistency. The culture we create now will echo far beyond our home.

I hope one day my kids can look back and say, "That makes more sense now—why he said that, why he did that, why he responded that way." My hope is that realization becomes an encouragement to them. Parenting often requires decisions children cannot fully understand in the moment. Clarity tends to come later. And that's okay.

Think of the best manager you've had. What made them effective? They were probably present and available, communicated expectations clearly, followed through consistently, collaborated when a better solution emerged, owned their mistakes, avoided micromanaging, and genuinely wanted you to succeed.

That's the posture parents should bring to chores and privileges.

What Great Managers Don't Do

Great managers do not

- remind endlessly,
- threaten vaguely,
- change rules emotionally,
- challenge beyond capacity,
- enforce consequences unpredictably, or
- shift expectations without notice.

When parents operate this way, chores become personal instead of formative. Kids stop learning responsibility and start managing emotions—often ours.

If it's hard for adults to relate to other adult leaders under these conditions, imagine how much harder it is for kids who are still developing to relate to adult leaders that struggle with poor leadership skills.

That's exhausting for everyone.

What Great Managers Do Instead

Great managers communicate clearly and make expectations clear.

In a healthy environment, people don't have to guess what success looks like. They know what is expected, when it is due, and how completion is measured. The same should be true for kids. They should be able to see their responsibilities clearly and understand how their work will be evaluated.

They also enforce consequences calmly and predictably. When work isn't completed, the response is straightforward in the home: "Your chore wasn't completed today, so one of your privileges is paused." No sermon. No sighing. No lecture. Just clarity.

This approach removes the parent from the emotional center of the system. The consequence isn't driven by frustration or mood; it flows from an agreed-upon structure. And structures are far easier to trust than emotions.

Over time, that steadiness builds security. Kids may not love the consequence, but they understand it, and they probably appreciate the reduction of lectures. And understanding reduces conflict far more effectively than intensity ever will.

One reason this matters even more in the home than in the workplace is that parents occupy multiple roles at once. We are nurturers, shepherds, friends, providers, supervisors, and coaches—often all in the same day. With that many roles overlapping, lines can blur quickly, and interactions can become unnecessarily personal.

As such, a clear system helps. It doesn't remove relationship, nor should it, but it does remove some of the emotional weight from everyday accountability. By externalizing expectations and consequences, the system provides clearer boundaries around the relationship, allowing parents to lead calmly and children to respond without feeling constantly evaluated.

Reacting Prematurely

In addition, a good manager doesn't react prematurely. They wait until it's clear an expectation truly wasn't met, or they ask a simple, clarifying question without hovering or micromanaging. The same principle applies at home.

When a chore isn't completed the way it was discussed, we don't jump on it immediately. In our home, all chores must be finished by 9:00 p.m. That time boundary matters. It allows parents to step back emotionally and allows children to manage their own time.

If 9:00 comes and goes and the chore still isn't done, we address it calmly—either that evening or the following morning, depending on the privilege involved.

For example: "Hey buddy, the dishes didn't get done by 9:00 p.m. last night. That means we're going to remove a privilege today. We'll also need to still get those dishes done."

Or, if it's just after the deadline: "It's after 9:00 p.m. and the dishes weren't finished, and you didn't mention needing more time to us. I just want to let you know we'll be taking a privilege tomorrow, and we'll still need the dishes done in the morning."

By waiting until the boundary has clearly passed, parents avoid getting pulled into debates at 8:55 p.m.: "I was just about to do them!" The system does the talking. You don't need to take it personally or argue your case.

And it doesn't have to be personal. The expectation remains. The chore still needs to be completed. If there's frustration or pushback afterward, that becomes a separate issue—often involving a separate privilege. Clear systems protect both authority and relationship.

Obviously, there will be exceptions. If people are coming over, plans change, or you simply want to move the timeline up for the day, that's fine—just communicate it early and give a reminder or two. When plans shift, reminders are completely appropriate.

At the same time, we want our kids to learn how to plan ahead. If they can see in advance that they may struggle to get their chores done on time and come talk with us about it, we're often willing to give a little flexibility.

For example, if our ten-year-old is invited to jump on the trampoline with his eight- and six-year-old siblings at dusk but still has some reading left, and he comes to us first and respectfully asks if it's okay to jump with his siblings a little longer even though he still needs to get the dishes done, we'll likely grant it.

The key lesson is that chores are not optional. There is room for negotiation when it's done politely and respectfully. But once it becomes a demand—or if they assume wiggle room is guaranteed simply because they asked—then it's no longer up for consideration.

What matters most is that everyone knows

- what is expected;
- when it is expected to be done; and
- how it is expected to be done.

Arguing and Consequences

A quick but important side note. In our home, if a privilege is removed because an agreed-upon responsibility wasn't completed, and the response of our children is arguing, debating, or escalating, another privilege is removed.

Our agreement is simple: In our home, parents aren't yelling and nagging about chores. In our home, kids aren't fighting back and arguing about chores. When expectations are clear and communicated ahead of time, consequences shouldn't feel surprising. They may feel disappointing—but not confusing.

Arguing after a clear consequence shifts the focus away from responsibility and toward power. It subtly trains children to believe that enough resistance might reverse a decision. We've decided that can't become part of our culture.

This doesn't mean our kids can't ask respectful questions. It doesn't mean they can't express some frustration. It means that once a decision has been made according to a structure we've already agreed on, **escalation carries its own consequence**.

In our home, a mostly calm response preserves dignity. Escalation compounds loss. And this only works because we hold up our end of the agreement.

In our home

- Parents don't raise their voices (with exceptions, like danger).
- Parents don't lecture and nag on chores.
- Parents don't punish impulsively.
- Parents follow through.

When our kids realize that arguing and escalation reliably leads to greater loss—and that calm responsibility restores trust—something shifts. Resistance decreases. Drama fades.

The key is saying less, not more. Staying steady isn't always easy for parents—and it isn't always easy for kids either. But teaching children that escalating when they're frustrated carries consequences is deeply formative. As children develop, they test limits in order to understand where boundaries exist. If boundaries aren't steady, they will keep testing until they find them.

In our home, escalation around incomplete chores has largely disappeared. Not because our kids are perfect—but because the boundaries are predictable. And as parents, we no longer react with raised voices or frustration when something isn't done on time or done correctly. That didn't happen overnight. There was a time when "I raised my voice because I had to" felt normal. It isn't anymore. The system steadied us. And over time, it steadied them.

Meaningful Changes Call for a Meaningful Meeting

When companies introduce a major change, they don't mention it in passing. They call a meeting. They explain what's changing, why it matters, how it affects everyone, and what to expect moving forward.

A chores plan is a meaningful change in the life of a home. It deserves the same level of intentionality.

Rolling it out formally communicates that this isn't reactive or emotional; it's thoughtful and structured. And interestingly, formal meetings can feel novel—even special—to kids. When parents prepare and gather everyone with purpose, children sense that something important is happening.

Before our meeting, we prepared carefully. We clarified

- what was happening in our home (ongoing conflict around chores)
- why change was necessary (we genuinely need your help)
- what was changing (chores will now connect directly to privileges)
- what the conditions would be (clear expectations and predictable consequences)
- what our shared commitment would look like (parents lead calmly; children follow through responsibly)

At first, this level of preparation felt unusually structured for family life. Then I realized we were simply applying principles businesses have used for decades: clarity, alignment, and shared expectations. Homes deserve that same clarity.

The plan itself was specific. Each child had defined chores assigned to particular days, clear deadlines, and a simple system for tracking completion. We prepared our tracking tool (Skylight, in our case) and knew exactly how it would function.

We considered what we would actually say, **trying to say no more than necessary**. Over-explaining to kids (especially younger ones) weakens clarity, and it's impossible to anticipate every question ahead of time. We explain things as simply as possible, and left space for questions to fill in the landscape.

Preparing for that meeting took a couple of hours. The clarity it created saved far more time—and far more conflict—later.

Before sitting down, we also thought through

- what privileges our children currently enjoyed
- which privileges would be paused if expectations weren't met
- what "incomplete" work actually meant
- how attitude and follow-through would be addressed
- when chores were due and how accountability would function
- the larger culture we were building

Putting the plan in writing mattered. It allowed us to lead calmly, reference a shared agreement, and avoid improvising in moments of frustration.

Guiding Principles for the Meeting and Starting the Plan

You've prepared the plan. Now the question is how to lead the conversation well and get started.

1. Let the meeting format communicate seriousness.

Before you say a word, the setting speaks. When you set aside time intentionally—free from distraction—and gather everyone with purpose, it communicates

- This matters.
- This isn't reactive.
- This is thoughtful.

For us, that meant scheduling it in advance and even setting the table with nice dishes, some donuts, and hot beverages (because nothing communicates maturity like a hot beverage).

Not because that's required, but because posture shapes perception. The meeting wasn't a lecture. It wasn't a scolding. It was a conversation about how our home would function moving forward.

2. Lead with calm clarity.

Tone matters more than detail.

If the meeting feels frustrated, kids hear resentment.

If it feels uncertain, they sense hesitation.

If it feels controlling, they brace themselves.

But when it feels calm and confident, they steady. A simple framing is enough: "We're making some changes in how our home runs.

This isn't because you're doing a bad job. It's because we want our home to work better—and we need your help."

3. Keep the "why" brief.

No over-explaining or lectures. You're not persuading with emotion; you're establishing structure. This isn't the "this is how life works" talk. It's the moment you design an environment that helps them experience how life works. Practice will connect the dots far more effectively than theory ever could.

Our "why" was this, "We know there is frustration around chores in the home, that we as parents maybe are nagging and yelling and getting frustrated, and also that things aren't usually done on time or completed properly. We want to help fix that, because we really need your help, and we don't want it to turn into an argument all the time."

This isn't the time for a long explanation about adulthood or how much other work parents do. Younger kids don't yet have the framework for that kind of lecture. The system itself becomes the framework.

Give them the watch. Don't explain how it works in microscopic detail.

4. Walk through expectations clearly.

Once the purpose is clear, outline

- what's expected;
- when it's due;
- how it's tracked; and
- how privileges connect to responsibility.

Invite questions—but don't open the floor to negotiation about whether responsibility is optional.

When fairness comes up (and it will), remind them that fairness doesn't mean sameness. As kids grow, both responsibility and privilege increase. Older kids may carry more chores—and often more freedom. Growth changes both sides of the equation.

Adjust for practical oversights if needed. But hold the structure steady. While rolling it out, we asked for questions, and we did end up modifying a couple of things after the kids voiced some of their thoughts. They raised something that made sense to adjust that we hadn't previously noticed.

But it wasn't really negotiation.

5. Start accountability immediately.

We rolled out our plan the moment the meeting ended. By design, most of our weekly chores were scheduled for Saturday morning after breakfast. So the meeting—also scheduled for Saturday—flowed directly into action.

There was no gap between explanation and implementation.

We worked alongside our kids that first day, walking through each chore together. When something was done incorrectly or incompletely, we addressed it in real time—not with frustration, but with clarity. We showed them what "complete" looked like. We demonstrated how to ask questions if they were unsure. We explained how to check off tasks properly.

Starting immediately prevented confusion and eliminated the gray space where momentum can stall. The system moved from theory to practice within minutes—and that made all the difference.

We gave our kids one week of practice—no privileges removed as long as they engaged without arguing and responded to feedback. We did the chores alongside them to demonstrate what "complete" looked like.

By week two, privileges were in play. Delaying accountability too long creates confusion. Consistent follow-through builds trust.

6. Hold steady through emotion.

Expect complaints at first. That's normal. A simple response works: "I get it. Nobody loves chores. But we're doing them. And this is how we're doing it."

Say less. Let the system do the work. Disappointment is allowed. Escalation is not. If arguing continues, that becomes part of the accountability structure you've already outlined. You can remind them, "We agreed you wouldn't fight us about this, and in return we agreed we won't raise our voices, lecture, or respond emotionally."

The key is steadiness. Pleasant. Calm. Predictable. Over time, that steadiness reduces resistance more effectively than intensity ever could.

Consequences That Teach Instead of Shame

One of the most important things parents need to hear is this: **consequences are not punishments**. Punishment is about retribution. Consequences are about formation.

Privileges being removed says two things:

1. Privileges are not a need. They are special, and we're glad you have them.

2. Privileges are earned and kept, but if they aren't helpful, they can be paused or lost.

The child experiences disappointment—but not rejection. They experience loss—but not shame. They learn—but they are not crushed.

And perhaps most importantly, the path forward is clear: Complete the responsibility, and in due time (soon!) regain the privilege. That clarity builds confidence over time. And they learn to value their privileges, which begins to cultivate gratitude. When something is earned and kept, it becomes more valuable.

Why This Protects the Relationship

Ironically, tying chores to privileges often *improves* the parent-child relationship. Why? Because expectations are no longer personal. They are structural. Parents become leaders again instead of referees. Kids stop trying to negotiate every outcome and start making choices within a known framework. That predictability creates peace. Kids may not always like the system, but they trust it.

Remember, we are living in an unusual era of privilege. The level of abundance before our children is unparalleled in human history. These circumstances require thoughtful approaches. When privilege is abundant, the line between needs and wants easily becomes blurred. By giving parts of this relationship clear structure, we help our children learn where those lines are.

One Step Further - Post the Plan in a Public Space

Taking one additional step can significantly strengthen a chores system: Create a written chores plan, walk through it together in a formal meeting, and treat it as a shared agreement.

This plan can be read together, discussed, clarified, and—if it fits your family's culture—signed. Older kids may benefit most from the act of signing, but younger kids can be included as well. The point isn't formality for its own sake; it's ownership. Signing simply reinforces that this isn't something being imposed in the moment; it's something that was agreed upon.

Once finalized, post the plan in a visible, shared place. Think of it like an HR document: not something referenced daily, but something available when questions or conflicts arise.

Day to day, your chore chart or Skylight will handle what's due. But when things don't go as planned—and when kids want to debate the ground rules—it's incredibly helpful to have a clear, written reference point. Instead of arguing, parents can calmly say, "Let's look at what we agreed on."

In practice, if expectations are clear and consistently held, you may find that you rarely need to reference the document at all. Most pushback isn't about confusion; it's about testing limits. And limits, when calmly and consistently enforced, tend to settle children rather than provoke them. We didn't implement this exact step in our own home, but we would if it came to that. A publicly posted, agreed-upon plan—with signatures if appropriate—removes ambiguity, reduces emotion, and allows the system to do its work.

And systems, as we've said, are far easier to trust than moods.

Quick Note on Ages

To be clear, in our home—with children ages six, eight, ten, and fifteen—we do not apply expectations in exactly the same way to every child.

Our six- and eight-year-olds are still learning rhythm, sequencing, and time awareness. Our six-year-old, in particular, genuinely enjoys chores. Our eight-year-old does not usually enjoy chores. When something is missed at that age, we usually offer a reminder, point them back to the system for reference, and give them space to correct it. If a chore is repeatedly skipped or left incomplete over time, we do apply a consequence—but not immediately. At that stage, our goal is learning, not pressure. We were careful not to create unnecessary anxiety.

Our ten- and fourteen-year-olds, on the other hand, understand expectations clearly. They know how the system works, what is required, and when things are due. At those ages, consistency matters more than reminders. The line can—and should—be held more firmly.

There is a point where children are fully capable of carrying responsibility without constant prompting, and that point arrives earlier than many parents expect. Even our younger two understand the system, and when it's time for chores, they generally step into it well.

The core principles remain the same at every age:

- Avoid nagging.
- Avoid lecturing.
- Avoid emotional or frustrated reactions.

For younger children, guidance comes first. For older children, follow-through comes faster. But in every case, if responsibilities are repeatedly ignored or completed poorly, a consequence is applied. The key is this: **Let the system do its work, not your emotions.**

Quick Note on Celebrating Chores

This may sound counterintuitive, but we don't celebrate chores in our house. No sticker charts. No rewards. No high fives. Usually not even a thank-you. Occasionally we'll express appreciation, but we don't make completion feel extraordinary. Chores are not a performance; they're participation.

The simple reality is this: Nobody loves chores. Not parents. Not kids. We all do them. The kids don't thank us for putting gas in the car, and we don't applaud them for emptying the dishwasher. We work together because we share a home together.

I say this carefully, because when your kids start completing chores without being asked, consistently, with a good attitude . . . something inside you will want to slay a fatted calf and celebrate. It feels incredible. Harmony in the home feels victorious. But I'd encourage you to resist turning that into ceremony.

The reward is the responsibility itself. There is something deeply formative about contributing without applause. It allows children to experience what it means to belong—to carry weight in a family simply because they are part of it.

That doesn't mean we never celebrate our kids. We celebrate growth, character, effort, kindness, creativity, courage. And if a child goes well beyond what was asked—if they take initiative or serve unexpectedly—we absolutely notice and say so.

But on an ordinary Tuesday night or Saturday morning, chores are just chores. The dishes are put away. The dog is walked. The trash is taken out. Good. The house functions the way it should. And then we move on.

What we have done, at times, is quietly mark a season with something fun. If the home has felt especially unified—if everyone has stepped up over weeks or months—we might surprise them with an outing or a special meal. Not as payment. Not as transaction. Just as gratitude for the overall spirit of the home. Daily tasks, though, remain ordinary. And that's the point.

Moving Toward Real Work

As kids grow, chores naturally lead toward work. They begin to notice things they want. They want money. They want independence. That desire is not a problem; it's an opportunity.

Paid jobs in and around the home allow kids to practice earning before they are ready for outside employment. Later, neighborhood jobs and part-time work extend those lessons into the real world.

Work teaches

- negotiation
- reliability
- humility
- effort
- social competence

It prepares kids for adulthood far more effectively than lectures ever could. This chapter intentionally stops at the point of moving into jobs and work that earn real money. Once kids begin working beyond chores and earning money, the next phase is helping them learn how to handle it—saving, spending, giving, and eventually investing. That deserves its own space, and we'll take it up next.

For now, the foundation is this: When kids experience real responsibility in the home, they become more grounded, more grateful, and more capable—and families often rediscover peace they thought was lost.

---

10 Key Takeaways

1. **Reframe chores as shared ownership.** Stop thinking of chores as "helping Mom and Dad." Begin framing them as participation in caring for a shared home. Use language like "we need you" rather than "help us."
2. **Define baseline chores vs. paid work.** Decide which responsibilities are
   - Baseline chores (required because you're part of the family; tied to privileges, not pay)
   - Optional jobs (extra work that can earn money)
   - Make this distinction explicit.
3. **Create a written chores plan.** Clarity now prevents conflict later. Write it all down:
   - Which accountability system (whiteboard, chores chart, Skylight)

- Each child's chores
- Which days they are responsible
- When chores are due
- What "completed" work looks like
- How chores connect to privileges

4. **Hold a formal family meeting.** Treat it like a real meeting, not a lecture. If needed, post the plan publicly. Don't roll out chores casually or mid-conflict. Set aside a dedicated time to
    - Explain *why* the plan exists
    - Walk through expectations
    - Answer questions calmly
5. **Make expectations visible.** This can be a chart, whiteboard, clipboard, or digital tool. The key is visibility and consistency, not the format. Use a system that allows kids to
    - See what's expected
    - Track their own completion
    - Know when something is missed
6. **Connect chores to privileges.** No lectures. Let the system speak. Identify privileges your children care about (screen time, social plans, gaming, phone access, etc.). Make it clear:
    - Privileges are not rights.
    - Privileges are kept through responsibility.
    - Privileges are lost when responsibilities aren't met.
7. **Apply consequences calmly and predictably.** State the outcome clearly: "The chore wasn't completed, so a privilege is paused." Consistency builds trust. When chores aren't completed:
    - Don't argue.
    - Don't lecture.
    - Don't react emotionally.
8. **Let the system—not your emotions—do the work.** Systems are easier to trust than moods. Avoid:
    - Nagging
    - Repeated reminders
    - Emotional escalation
9. **Adjust expectations by age, not personality.** Younger kids need guidance and reminders. Older kids need consistency and follow-through. Different approaches, same system.

10. **Review and update the plan periodically**. Between reviews, hold the plan steady. Revisit the plan every few months to
    - Adjust chores as kids grow
    - Clarify expectations
    - Reaffirm shared ownership
    - Post in a public space

Chapter 11

Working and Earning Money

It is critical that kids be engaged with chores. Most parents instinctively know this. Where families tend to diverge is *how* chores are connected to money. Some parents choose the Dave Ramsey–style approach, assigning a price tag to every chore so kids earn money for every chore. Other families use allowances, sometimes tied to chores and sometimes not.

In our home, we landed somewhere different. We didn't feel that the baseline responsibilities of family life were optional. Because of that, we weren't comfortable paying our kids for them. Instead, we chose to tie chores to privileges, not pay. That decision became one of the most formative shifts we made.

By connecting privileges to a baseline of responsibility, we accomplished two things at once. First, we clarified that contributing to the home is simply part of being in the family. Second, we gave privileges real weight. They became something to keep—and something that could be lost. And it was no longer arbitrary, it was by design. They lost privileges before too, but it wasn't well measured.

No system is perfect, but this approach made a massive difference for us.

Just the other night, a chore was overlooked. The next morning, I brought it up to one of our older boys who was responsible for it. I said, "Hey, you know what that means today, right?"

He replied, "Yeah. No screens today."

Then I asked, "And you still need to finish the chore, right?"

"Yep. I'll do it now."

That was it.

No argument. No escalation. No dread on my part about confronting the issue. If you had seen this same interaction play out a couple of years ago, you would have marveled at the difference.

This is the foundation. Chores and privileges form **Phase One**. But this chapter is really about **Phase Two**—what happens when responsibility matures into work and earning.

Wanting More Is Not Necessarily the Problem

Everybody wants stuff. You do. I do. Our kids definitely do. Kids ask for things constantly. And while that can feel exhausting to parents—nails on a chalkboard at times—it's actually the perfect teaching moment for one of the most important lessons they will ever learn.

Here it is: **If you want something you don't have, and it isn't a need, then you need to work for it.** Now that's something Dave Ramsey and I can agree on! That idea may sound obvious. But in a culture where so much arrives without effort, it's becoming far less intuitive than we think.

In the same way that tying chores to privileges helps children connect effort to *keeping* the good things they already have, earning money for other wants helps them connect effort to *getting* new things they desire. As children grow, their world expands. Their desires become more specific. They want independence, autonomy, and choice. And eventually, they want money—not just a few dollars here and there, but enough to meaningfully pursue the things that matter to them.

Chores and Jobs Are Not the Same Thing in Our Home

One of the most important distinctions we make in our home—and one that families often miss—is differentiating between **chores** and **jobs**. Call them whatever you want. In our house, chores are unpaid responsibilities required because you belong to the family. Jobs are optional opportunities to earn money.

Chores are required. Jobs are optional. Chores exist because family life is shared life. They are not negotiated, not dependent on mood, and not transactional. Jobs exist for a different reason. They exist to create opportunity. A child chooses to work because they want something beyond what the family already provides.

This distinction is foundational. When everything is paid, kids can simply opt out of work when motivation dips—especially around birthdays, holidays, or seasons when money flows freely. Work loses its meaning, and parents wonder why motivation disappears.

Separating chores from jobs keeps the system honest. Life requires responsibility even when no one is paying you. But work creates opportunity when you want more. That is how adulthood works.

Household Jobs: Training Wheels for the Real World

When kids are younger, the home is the best place to practice earning. Household jobs function like training wheels. They allow children to learn what it means to work for pay while parents are still close enough to coach, clarify expectations, and help them recover from mistakes.

These jobs are not allowances (but allowances are okay, too!). They are not automatic. They are not guaranteed. They are offered when work needs to be done and a child wants to earn.

For us, examples include deep-cleaning projects, organizing storage spaces, yard work, seasonal tasks, laundry for other members of the family, or one-time projects that go beyond baseline chores. For us, cleaning all the LEGOs off a floor of a room where all the kids play is a great one. Anyone can do it, nobody wants to.

At this stage, parents still play an active role. You help define what "done" looks like. You clarify timelines. You may correct quality. But you resist rescuing. The job becomes the teacher. Children learn that earning requires follow-through, that incomplete work earns incomplete pay, and that reliability matters. These lessons stick because they are *experienced*, not explained.

For example, mowing the yard in our home earns $10. That includes mowing the front and back yards, trimming the edges, and blowing off the sidewalk. If part of the job is skipped, the pay is reduced accordingly. The standard is clear, and so is the outcome.

In another case, our teenager does the laundry for his siblings and himself for $20 per week. He's happy to do it because the income is predictable. The expectation, however, is specific: His siblings' clothes must be folded and put away by 6:00 p.m. on Sunday. His own laundry isn't held to that deadline, but theirs is. If the job isn't completed on time, the pay drops to $10.

There are exceptions. Life happens. But the rule of thumb is simple: Exceptions are negotiated *in advance*. When our kids communicate early and reasonably, we're generous with flexibility. When they don't, the original agreement stands.

Beyond weekly work, we're glad to pay for one-time jobs—shoveling snow off the driveway, deep cleaning a room, organizing a closet, hauling items, clearing yard debris, washing or vacuuming cars. These tasks go beyond baseline family responsibilities and create opportunities to earn.

Over time, kids begin to understand essential things: Pay is tied to completion, communication matters, and reliability builds trust. That's not a lecture about work ethic; it's a lived experience of how the world actually works.

Kids also learn that opportunities don't always wait for perfect timing. Sometimes a job needs to be done, no one takes it, and we handle it ourselves. A few days later, when a child decides they want something badly enough to work for it, the opportunity is gone.

They also learn that effort and reliability create opportunity. When one child consistently does good work with a willing attitude, we naturally offer them more chances. That isn't favoritism; it's how trust works. Over time, children see that showing up well leads to more responsibility and greater opportunity.

This creates a healthy form of motivation. Optional work may be available, but it isn't always optimal if a child wants to earn more. Kindness, humility, and a readiness to help when work is offered all matter. Those qualities don't just make family life run more smoothly—they shape how opportunity works in the real world. There are limits, of course, but the kids understand the framework. It makes sense to them.

One of our kids is generally content not taking on many extra jobs. Another looks for as many opportunities as possible. The others tend to step forward when they want something that costs extra. Each interacts with the system differently, but all of them understand the principle. If they want something that isn't a need—and it isn't a birthday or Christmas—it's time to work.

When the Home Is No Longer Enough

Eventually—and this is important—the home should no longer be able to meet a child's financial wants. As kids move into adolescence, their desires naturally grow. At that point, it is neither healthy nor appropriate for household jobs to fund potentially hundreds of dollars a month of wants—unless you're running a business out of your home, and they're working for the family business. That would be different, of course.

The home is not meant to be a long-term employer. This creates an intentional fork in the road:

Either the family funds the desire, or the child steps into real work outside the home to supplement.

That fork is one of the most formative moments in childhood.

Stepping Outside the Home Requires Courage

Working outside the home introduces lessons children cannot learn inside family systems alone. They must ask for work, handle rejection, show up on time, take instruction from adults who aren't emotionally invested in them, and receive feedback that may be blunt.

Neighborhood jobs often serve as the bridge—babysitting, lawn care, pet sitting, snow removal, helping small businesses. Part-time jobs follow. Parents should normalize this step, not with pressure but with clarity: "There's nothing necessarily wrong with wanting more. But wanting more means you'll need to work outside of the home for much of it." That framing honors desire while anchoring it in responsibility.

Why Parents Should Not Pay Full Market Rates

Parents should not try to out-pay the real world. If the home pays more than outside work, kids will stay home. If the home shields kids from difficulty, they will avoid real work. The goal is not to make work comfortable. The goal is to make work real.

Outside work pays differently because it demands more from them in the way of inconvenience; they're working with people they don't necessarily know super well, who may not be as flexible, who communicate differently. And they probably pay more. When kids experience that difference, they begin to understand how value is created. That understanding produces humility and perspective.

Now, if you have your own business your kids can be involved in, maybe that's a little different. But typically, you will want to pay discounted rates for work in the home.

Work Builds Dignity

When children work to earn money, their relationship with value changes. What they want becomes something to pursue, not request. Because of that, they tend to value what they earn more, care for it more carefully, and think longer before spending.

At the same time, work itself takes on greater meaning. Tasks are approached with more care because effort now leads to a visible outcome they care about.

Over time, earning also teaches that not all work carries the same value. Some work earns more because it requires greater skill, responsibility, or reliability. As children experience this difference, they begin to understand why growth and learning matter—and why certain kinds of work create more opportunity.

Ideally, children begin to look for work they enjoy and that also pays well. But work offers far more than income. It builds dignity. It builds self-trust. It builds relationship with people they otherwise probably wouldn't be rubbing shoulders with. It teaches children that they can carry weight—that they are capable and needed.

In our home, I want our kids to learn this *before* they choose a college or a trade—before they finish high school. After high school, in my mind, is the right time to begin exploring specialization: taking first steps toward a career or, just as importantly, learning early what they *don't* want to do while they still have freedom to change direction.

My teenager had been off and on about finding work outside the home. About a year ago, I encouraged him again. He hesitated. Weeks later, we attended a neighborhood gathering in our cul-de-sac. Sam struck up a conversation with an older neighbor, and the two connected. The neighbor mentioned—almost casually—that he *might* need some help with yard work. Sam didn't hesitate.

That small opening became something meaningful. This neighbor, now in his eighties, relies on Sam for mowing, weed trimming, moving things, cleaning up—whatever needs doing. Sam shows up ready, dependable, and willing. Over time, he's grown confident in that role, and he's learned to value the relationship as much as the paycheck. He's ready when our neighbor reaches out for really just about anything.

It's hard to imagine a better confidence-builder at this stage of his life than knowing a neighbor genuinely needs him—and is willing to pay him for good work. The relationship matters to both of them, and that's one of the quiet gifts of helping kids learn to work early. They don't just earn money. They experience the fabric of real life—where contribution, trust, and relationship are woven together. It's going to look different for every kid. What's meaningful for each child will be varied.

As Rachel Cruze, daughter of Dave Ramsey and coauthor of *Smart Money, Smart Kids*, regularly points out, "Without fail, every time I'm on the road speaking to groups, I have a parent ask me, 'How can I raise my kids not to feel entitled? How can I teach them the value of a dollar?' From my experience, the basic principle of working is one of the best ways to combat the attitude of entitlement."[44] We should be motivated to help our kids engage in real work outside of the home!

Healthy Limits Still Matter

Work is formative—but not all work is equally formative at every age. Teenagers still need margins. They need sleep, school engagement, family rhythms, friendships, faith, and rest. When work crowds those things out, it stops forming and starts taking.

That's why parents must stay involved, even as kids gain independence. The goal is not fast-tracking adulthood. The goal is steady preparation for it. Good limits protect character, preserve relationships, and allow responsibility to grow without overwhelming the child. It's good for our kids to be eager to work, but it's important that there are limits prior to them finishing high school and being engaged during that season of life.

Some students may consider stepping away from extracurricular school activities in order to work. That decision isn't inherently right or wrong; it depends on context and motivation. What matters most is why they're making the choice. That's where parental presence is essential: helping them examine their motives, weigh trade-offs, and make decisions rooted in growth rather than impulse.

Types of Work to Be Cautious About

Not all jobs that a teenager can get are good jobs. Getting a job where they have a friend may or may not be a good idea. Work environments to be cautious about include

- **Jobs with late-night hours** that consistently interfere with sleep, school, or family rhythms
- **Highly adult environments** where teens are exposed early to

coarse language, unhealthy social dynamics, or pressures they are not equipped to navigate
- **Jobs where they are standing around** for large chunks at a time, scrolling on their phones (this probably isn't productive work for them to have)

This doesn't mean teens must be sheltered indefinitely. Just as we don't hand car keys to a ten-year-old because they can reach the pedal, we shouldn't assume every job is appropriate simply because a teen is eager or capable.

Parents should think less in terms of *prestige* or *pay* and more in terms of environment and formation. A good early job usually includes

- clear expectations;
- accountability;
- reasonable supervision; and
- opportunities to learn from mistakes without severe consequences.

How Many Hours Is Enough?

More work is not always better work. Teenagers need margin. They need enough space for school and adequate sleep, for family rhythms and friendships, for spiritual formation, and for the kind of unstructured rest that allows them to recover and think clearly. When work begins to crowd out those essentials, it stops forming responsibility and starts creating imbalance.

A helpful rule of thumb that many experts agree on is

Younger teens: Limited hours, often seasonal or part-time (five to ten hours per week)

Older teens: Increased responsibility, but still capped (ten to fifteen, occasionally up to twenty hours per week)

Once work begins to regularly exceed those ranges during the school year, parents should pause and reassess. Questions worth asking include

- Is this job supporting or undermining school engagement?
- Is it creating fatigue or stress?
- Is it crowding out family or faith commitments?
- Is my teen growing in responsibility—or just surviving the schedule?
- Work should add structure, not chaos.

Why Parents Must Still Set Limits

One of the hardest parts of this phase is knowing when to say no—especially when a teenager wants more hours or more money. Teens often equate more work with more independence. Parents can feel torn between encouraging responsibility and protecting balance.

This is where parental leadership still matters. Teenagers do not yet have the perspective to see long-term trade-offs clearly. They feel immediate benefits more strongly than future costs. Parents, on the other hand, are called to hold the *whole picture*. Setting limits on work hours or types of work is not controlling; it is guiding. You're saying, "I'm for you working. I'm not for work owning you."

Work Should Expand Responsibility, Not Replace It

Work should expand a teen's sense of responsibility, not replace it. If a teen begins working and suddenly

- chores disappear,
- family contribution stops,
- responsibilities at home vanish,
- then work has become an escape, not a growth opportunity.

A healthy posture sounds more like, "Now that you're working, you'll need to manage *both* your job and your responsibilities at home." This mirrors adult life. Work doesn't excuse us from caring for our homes, relationships, or obligations. It requires better management of them.

If the School Year Is Limited, Then Summer Is the Jackpot

We've been talking primarily about working during the school year—and maybe that's right for your child, or maybe it isn't. Based on my own experience working through high school, and the research I've done since, I'm not convinced that holding a job during the school year is essential for every teenager.

Summer, however, is a different story. Summertime offers a unique window for meaningful work and earning. With fewer academic demands and more unstructured hours, kids have space to work toward clear financial goals—whether through neighborhood jobs, family connections, or seasonal positions that naturally open up during the summer months.

Beth Kobliner offers a practical guideline that supports this focus on summer, and even goes a little further: "My advice: If it's feasible, have your kid skip the after-school job and focus on making money over the summer instead. Of course, if he wants to pick up occasional odd jobs such as babysitting or tutoring, that's great, as long as they don't eat into homework time."[45]

Kobliner isn't discouraging work. Rather, she is guiding families to balance three realities:

- Earning builds responsibility and connection to provision;
- school and cognitive formation still matter; and
- work should not overwhelm the rhythms that support long-term growth.

Kids can learn a great deal from meaningful, seasonal work without undermining their responsibilities to school, family, or character growth. Even occasional, self-initiated jobs—like babysitting or tutoring—can build initiative and confidence.

Summer work channels downtime in a constructive direction. Is there something significant they want to save for? Could you motivate them by matching a portion of what they earn? Used well, summer becomes a rare jackpot—an opportunity for kids to build discipline, confidence, and ownership, all while learning what it means to earn and steward money.

Moving into Earning Money

Earning money is the first threshold—but it is not the finish line. Once children begin to earn, a new and equally important phase begins: learning how to handle money with wisdom and restraint. Saving, spending, giving, and planning all introduce something children rarely learn naturally: delayed gratification.

For now, the foundation is this:

- Chores teach responsibility.
- Jobs teach agency.
- Outside work builds courage and independence.

Together, these experiences form children who understand that effort precedes reward—and who are far less vulnerable to entitlement and far more prepared for adulthood. The next chapter takes the next step: how to help children allocate what they earn in ways that shape patience, purpose, and long-term thinking by developing financial literacy.

When children earn money by contributing effort—whether through chores, part-time jobs, or meaningful tasks around the home—they begin to connect effort with provision. This simple principle helps move them from expecting provision by default to understanding the dignity and responsibility that come with earning, stewarding, and managing money.

---

12 Key Takeaways

1. Foundational Distinctions
    - Chores and jobs are not the same thing (by Doug's definition).
        - Chores = unpaid responsibilities because you belong to the family.
        - Jobs = optional opportunities to earn money because you want more.
    - Tie chores to privileges, not pay.
    - Use jobs to teach earning, agency, and initiative.
2. Phase Two: Work → Earning
    - Teach this core rule early and often: "If you want something that isn't a need, you need to work for it."
    - Don't rush to fund children's wants for them.
    - View desire for more as an opportunity, not a problem.
3. Using Household Jobs Well
    - Treat household jobs as training wheels for real work outside the home.
    - Jobs should be
        - optional;
        - clearly defined;
        - time-bound; and
        - paid only when completed well.
    - Define what "done" looks like before the job starts.
    - Reduce pay for incomplete or late work.
    - Allow flexibility only when negotiated in advance.
4. What Kids Learn Through Earning
    - Follow-through matters.
    - Incomplete work earns reduced pay.
    - Reliability builds trust.
    - Opportunity is not guaranteed; it must be seized.
5. Opportunity and Motivation
    - If work is available and no one takes it, let it go.
    - Give more opportunities to kids who

        - show up consistently;
        - do quality work; and
        - carry a willing attitude.
    - This is not favoritism; it's how trust works. If a child has been slow to take ownership of their responsibilities but later finds the motivation to step up, take the time to revisit it with them.
6. When the Home Is No Longer Enough
    - As kids get older, household jobs should not fund all their wants.
    - Create a natural fork in the road:
        - parents fund the desire, or
        - child steps into outside work.
    - Hold this boundary calmly.
7. Stepping Outside the Home
    - Normalize outside work as a healthy next step.
    - Neighborhood jobs often come first (babysitting, yard work, pet care).
    - Outside work teaches
        - initiative;
        - rejection;
        - accountability;
        - humility; and
        - courage.
8. Pay Wisely
    - Keep home pay lower than outside work.
    - Let kids experience why some work pays more than others.
9. Work Builds Dignity
    - Earning changes how kids value
        - money;
        - effort; and
        - possessions.
    - Work builds
        - confidence;
        - self-trust;
        - competence; and
        - perspective.
    - The goal is formation, not income.
10. Keep Healthy Limits

- Work should not replace
  - school engagement;
  - sleep;
  - family rhythms; and
  - faith formation.
- Suggested school-year ranges:
  - Younger teens: ~5–10 hours/week.
  - Older teens: ~10–15 (occasionally up to 20) hours/week.
- Reassess if work creates stress or chaos.

11. Choose Work Environments Carefully
    - Be cautious with
      - late-night jobs;
      - highly adult environments; and
      - low-accountability, high-idle-time jobs.
    - Look for
      - clear expectations;
      - supervision; and
      - room to learn from mistakes.
12. Don't Let Work Replace Responsibility
    - A job does not excuse kids from
      - chores;
      - family contribution; and
      - homework.
    - Teach kids to manage both work and home responsibilities.

Chapter 12

Financial Literacy—Part 1: Developing Delayed Gratification

The moment kids begin earning money, something important changes. Earning introduces possibility. Money in the hands of a child can become a powerful teacher—or a quiet distorter, depending on how it is handled. Without structure, money trains impulse. With structure, it trains restraint.

This chapter is the first step in developing financial literacy. Before children learn about budgets, investing, or long-term planning, they must first learn something more basic and more formative: how to allocate what they earn. Allocation means intentionally dividing money into categories such as spending, saving, giving, and eventually investing. This simple habit shapes financial behavior at its roots. It teaches children that money is not meant to be consumed all at once, that choices involve trade-offs, and that meaningful goals often require waiting.

In that sense, allocation teaches delayed gratification and self-control. These are not merely financial skills. They are life skills that shape how children relate to desire, effort, and responsibility over time.

The reason this topic deserves its own chapter is that while the idea is simple in theory, it can be more challenging in practice. Personalities differ. Families handle allowances and earnings differently. Children drift from plans, savings goals shift, and giving can easily be forgotten without intentional structure. But a thoughtful plan goes a long way. With a few clear rhythms in place, money becomes one of the most practical tools for teaching responsibility, patience, and gratitude.

Why Allocation Matters More Than Amount

The primary goal of allocation is not saving money arbitrarily; it is **developing delayed gratification**, the ability to wait for a better future reward instead of taking something smaller right now. Research consistently shows that delayed gratification in childhood is linked to stronger emotional regulation, healthier decision-making, and greater long-term stability in adulthood.

Allocation creates a pause between earning and spending. That pause is where growth happens. Many parents worry that allocation will frustrate their kids or make money feel overly controlled. In practice, the opposite is usually true.

Allocation actually *protects* kids from themselves.

Children are not wired yet for long-term thinking. They are wired for immediacy. As such, if all the money that comes in can be used for whatever they want, it sets a certain type of habit in place. However, if the money that comes in is understood to have a purpose, and some of that (but not all of it) is enjoyment now, then we are setting our kids up for greater self-control.

When kids earn money we should help them understand that every dollar a child earns should have a purpose.

1. Give—to develop generosity.
2. Save—to prepare for future needs.
3. Spend—to enjoy appropriate wants.
4. Invest—to grow resources over time.

These four categories train children to see money not just as something to consume, but as something to steward.

Money Is Like Electricity

Electricity is powerful with enormous potential. When governed well, it quietly powers almost every part of life. When left unregulated, it becomes dangerous—not because electricity is bad, but because power without direction is destructive.

The reason electricity safely runs through our homes is simple: it is governed. The electrical panel does not reduce the power entering the house; it directs it, limits it, and protects everything it powers. Without that panel, the same electricity that lights a room could burn the house down. Money works much the same way.

Money itself is not inherently good or evil. But it is powerful. And when it is left unchecked, it can quietly reshape priorities, relationships, and desires. Jesus says plainly, "No one can serve two masters. . . . You cannot serve God and money" (Matthew 6:24 NIV). Money is not presented as evil, **but as a rival.**

A force powerful enough to demand allegiance if left unchecked. Paul echoes the same warning, cautioning that the love of money can lead people into traps and misplaced hope, urging believers instead to place their trust in God, who richly provides all things to enjoy (1 Timothy 6:9–10, 17–19). The issue is not possession, but direction. Not income, but governance.

Money quietly shapes parts of our lives whether we notice it or not. And that power does not suddenly appear when we turn eighteen. It has always been there.

Giving Kids Good Wiring

When kids learn early that money is meant to be directed, not simply spent, they gain a quiet advantage that can spare them significant confusion later in life.

By giving children structure around money, we are not restricting them; we are protecting them. We are installing the electrical panel before the power increases. We are helping them develop the internal wiring—a healthy operating system—needed to steward responsibility wisely, delay gratification, and live free from being mastered by the very tools meant to serve them and others.

This does not mean they will avoid mistakes. But when mistakes happen, there is a framework to return to—a familiar system that allows them to recalibrate rather than start over. Structure gives children a place to reset, rather than unravel.

Delayed Gratification Is the Gift

When we teach our kids healthy habits around money—how it can serve both them and others—we give them one of the greatest developmental gifts: delayed gratification.

Delayed gratification is the ability to manage impulses and orient behavior toward future goals. Research across multiple fields shows that children who develop stronger self-control and patience tend to experience better outcomes later in life—stronger educational achievement, greater financial stability, better health, and fewer behavioral problems. In many studies, these traits predict life outcomes as strongly as, or more strongly than, intelligence. [46,47,48]

Importantly, delayed gratification is not simply a personality trait or a matter of raw willpower. It is part of a set of skills often called *executive functioning*—abilities like impulse control, planning ahead, and staying focused—that develop through practice over time.

Children learn these skills best in environments that are consistent and trustworthy, where expectations are clear and boundaries are reliable. This reinforces a central theme of this book: Self-control is not formed through lectures or pressure, but through structure and repeated practice in everyday life.

Teaching children to allocate what they earn creates hundreds of small opportunities to practice this skill. Each time a child chooses not to spend immediately, they rehearse a deeper truth: *Not everything I want needs to be satisfied right now.* Over time, this ability strengthens nearly every area of life.

A Child's Relationship with Money

Like an electrical panel in a home, allocation separates money into distinct pathways—spending, saving, giving, and eventually investing—each with a purpose and a limit. When children learn to allocate money, they begin to see it not as something to consume immediately but as something to steward.

At first, this structure may feel restrictive. That is normal. Structure almost always feels limiting before it begins to feel empowering. But that resistance fades when children begin to experience the results; when savings grow, generosity takes shape, or a long-awaited purchase finally becomes possible because they planned for it. I've watched that transition happen repeatedly in our own home. My kids no longer push against the system. They operate within it naturally.

Here's one story about my second-born son, Max, who is now ten.

A Quick Story – The System Teaches the Lesson

When our son Max was nine, he experienced one of those small moments that quietly shapes a lifetime.

Max had been earning money and allocating it consistently. He understood the system: part went into spending, part into saving, part into giving.

On one particular outing, Max walked into a sports cards store with a spending envelope he only planned on spending a little money from. Once he was in that store with his siblings and things got exciting, he spent every last dollar of his spending money. We were fine with that; we celebrate when they spend that money. That's part of our system. On this day, it was Pokémon and sports cards.

At first, there was excitement. For hours, he enjoyed himself. He'd made his choice freely. No one stopped him. That money was his, and he spent it. But the next morning, the emotional shift came. Regret set in. The thrill faded, replaced by that familiar feeling we all know too well: *I wish I had thought about that a little longer.*

Then something remarkable happened. Max remembered his savings. It was really interesting what unfolded next. He came into my office at home, eyes wide, sauntering slowly like he had seen a ghost. He approached my desk quietly, took a few seconds, and said, "Dad. I didn't plan on spending all my spending envelope money yesterday, but I did. I was hoping actually that I would put some of that money toward my fishing rod I was saving for."

And then there was a pause. "But then I remembered this morning I still have my savings envelope with money set aside for the fishing rod . . . [moment of silence and contemplation] . . . I'm so glad I have that envelope." And then he left. And that was it. Relief washed over him as he saw why we set money aside for future better goals, intentionally.

The money he had been working toward—**the future goal**—was still there. He hadn't failed. He had simply learned. That combination—**regret paired with relief**—is extraordinarily formative. It teaches a lesson no lecture ever could. Max learned, in real time, that spending impulsively carries emotional weight, and that saving creates stability. He felt both sides of the equation in his own body, in his own experience.

We didn't rescue him. We didn't shame him. We didn't adjust the rules. The system did exactly what it was designed to do. Actually, I never even said anything. I recently asked Max if he remembered that moment so I could have his permission to put it in this book, and he barely remembers it. But that day, the principle was galvanized in a way where words weren't even needed.

Also, he went broke on one envelope but not on all his envelopes. He realized he had made a mistake but that a guardrail was in place that protected his other goals.

And that's the point. When kids are allowed to spend their spending money freely—with some healthy exceptions (i.e., candy has a limit!)—they begin to internalize wisdom rather than borrowing it from their parents. Over time, those small moments add up. They learn to pause. They learn to plan. They learn that not every dollar needs to be spent immediately, and that protecting the future feels better than satisfying every impulse in the present.

Max didn't just learn how money works that day. He learned how *he* works. And that is the deeper goal of allocation.

A Simple Approach

Helping our kids allocate their earned money doesn't have to be complicated. Far from it. But like chores and technology, it needs to have some clear boundaries and guiding principles to make it work smoothly.

The Non-Negotiable Principle: Allocate the Same Day

If there is one practice parents should treat as non-negotiable, it is this:

When your kids earn money at home, pay them the same day and help them separate and allocate it the same day. Not tomorrow. Not "when we get around to it." The day money is earned is when the lesson is strongest. Delay weakens the connection between effort and intention.

Allocating the same day

- interrupts impulse;
- normalizes division;
- reinforces habit over emotion; and
- removes negotiation.

Common Allocation Splits (and Why the Percentages Matter Less Than the Habit)

Many parents want to know what the "right" percentage split is. Honestly, I know parents who have succeeded with wildly different splits. The percentages matter far less than consistency. The goal is not optimization; it is repetition. That said, having a starting framework helps families move forward confidently.

Here are the allocation splits we use:

- **Younger kids**: 50% spending / 40% saving / 10% giving
- **Older kids and teens**: 40% spending / 40% saving / 10% giving / 10% investing

These are not moral formulas. They are training wheels. Over time, families may adjust based on age, maturity, or income. What should not change is the habit of dividing money every time it is earned.

One of the most important mindset shifts for parents deliberating how much should be spent or saved is realizing that **the saved money will eventually be spent anyway**. When kids understand this, resistance often disappears. Allocation is not about deprivation; it is about pacing.

I know some folks who do 80% into spending, 10% into saving, and 10% into giving. Or 70/10/10/10 with that last 10% for investing.

I let my kids spend half of their money with virtually NO input from me. The reality is that saving money is going to get spent too, just later. I love seeing them save toward goals, and I enjoy seeing them spend a chunk of money when it's there. I'm not worried about them making super smart spending decisions right now; I'm focused on them learning to wire their system with intention and create boundaries with money.

I could certainly add more layers here—teaching detailed budgeting or tracking every dollar. But at this stage, for me, that isn't the goal. The aim is simpler and more foundational: to help children regularly flex the muscle of money allocation whenever money comes into their hands.

When money shows up, it isn't meant to be consumed automatically. It is meant to be **allocated**. That repeated practice—deciding in advance where money goes—forms the muscle that later supports budgeting, planning, and wise financial decision-making.

Systems for Allocation: Choosing What Fits Your Family

There is no single "right" system. There is only a system you will actually use. There are three primary categories of systems, each appropriate at different developmental stages.

1. Physical Systems: Jars and Boxes

For younger kids, money needs to be visible and tangible. Jars and save/spend/give boxes allow kids to

- see money move;
- touch it;

- count it; and
- feel the difference between categories.

These systems are simple, inexpensive, and effective. They slow spending naturally and make saving feel real.

Parents act as the bank—breaking bills, making change, and helping kids track balances. This involvement creates natural conversation and oversight.

2. Transitional Systems: Envelopes with Parental Oversight

As children grow, the way they manage money needs to mature with them. For many families, envelopes become a helpful transition between simple jars and more adult financial tools. They are portable, flexible, and closer to how money actually functions in the real world. In that sense, envelopes often represent a "sweet spot"—simple enough for kids to understand, but structured enough to teach restraint and planning.

Envelopes also introduce realism. Because they are portable, children learn to plan ahead. They can see what they have available, what they've already committed to saving, and what remains for discretionary use. Many parents who have used envelope systems themselves recognize this benefit immediately—clarity reduces friction, and structure simplifies decision-making.

In our own home, envelopes became a natural next step as our kids grew older and their financial world expanded. There was a time when Ashley and I used envelopes. Eventually we moved to multiple checking accounts and debit cards that were auto-paid up each month because everything became more digital.

What mattered most was not the tool itself, but the habits it reinforced: planning before spending, accepting limits, and learning to wait.

Transitional systems are training tools. Envelopes help children practice governing money in a concrete, manageable way so that, when more complex tools are introduced later, the underlying habits are already in place.

3. Digital Systems: Greenlight and Similar Platforms

For kids roughly age ten and up, digital systems (like a debit card) begin to make sense—especially as money in the real world becomes increasingly cashless.

Among digital tools, there are actually quite a few family money management apps with debit cards, but Greenlight is our favorite. They are all pretty similar, but Greenlight has (in my opinion) a bit more intuition built into their application for families and especially related to sub-accounts.

A Closer Look at Greenlight: Why It Works So Well

Greenlight is not simply a debit card for kids. It is a **digital allocation system for a family with built-in guardrails**, which makes it particularly effective for teaching self-control.

Parents open a Greenlight account, add money to the Parent Wallet, and then add their kids to the account, and it is then easy to add or take money from the kids' Greenlight accounts, which each have a debit card, and if they have a phone they can see exactly what is in their account.

Key features that support formation:

- Sub-accounts for spending, saving, giving, and investing
- No overdraft protection (transactions decline if funds aren't available)
- Real-time parent notifications
- Full transaction history
- Multiple child profiles under one parent account

These features do something critical: They let natural consequences do the teaching. It is the digital envelope system of family finances for kids.

Greenlight also supports

- QR code payment links for receiving payment with integration to Google Pay and Apple Pay
- Venmo, but only (currently) as a source of funds from their own (or your own) Venmo
- easy replacement of lost cards
- controlled exposure to digital spending without full banking complexity

For many families, Greenlight functions better than a traditional checking account during the pre-employment years. It mirrors adult systems while preserving oversight.

Although it's not officially a checking account, it acts just like one, but without all the cumbersome nature of having to have separate sign-in, account fees, etc.

Investing Through Greenlight: Exposure Without Pressure

One of the most compelling uses of Greenlight is its investing component for teens. Our teenager puts part of his allocated earnings into his investing account on his phone app whenever he earns money.

Investing through Greenlight allows parents to

- introduce long-term thinking;
- compare individual stocks with index funds;
- teach diversification over time; and
- discuss volatility in real terms.

Simple practices—like waiting until $25 accumulates before investing—creates rhythm without urgency. We let that money build as cash in the investment sub-account on Greenlight, and each time it reaches $25, we invest it.

At first, the kids choose companies they think are interesting. They watch prices move up and down. Over time, something predictable happens: they start asking questions. "What would you invest in?" And that opens the door to a bigger conversation about long-term thinking, diversification, and efficient investments. The habit comes first. The sophistication comes later.

When we opened his investing account option on Greenlight, we spent fifteen to twenty minutes talking about how money grows over time IF it is invested well, and how it doubles over time based on the "Rule of 72." That blew his mind and gave him enough reason to understand why he would begin investing today.

Less is more.

Spending

In our experience, kids should be free to spend their spending money—even poorly. Regret is a better teacher than lectures. Over time, freedom paired with limits leads to better choices. We have limits on things like candy and things that aren't good for them, but really, if they want to spend $3 on a soda at the hockey rink when they're at their sibling's hockey game, I'll let them. It usually happens once or twice and then the novelty wears off.

Or $10 on some toy that's going to break in a day or two, sure. We celebrate that spend. Sometimes if we "know" they came into a store hoping to buy something else we may remind them as a courtesy, but we don't try to "teach" them about how to spend their money. They figure it out. Especially if they've had to work for it.

Savings

Our kids are required to have a "savings goal" listed on their jar or envelope, so they can remember what they are saving for and how much it costs, so they know when they reach their goal. In Greenlight, they can have several savings goals with amounts that they work toward.

We allow the kids to change their goal, but it needs to be thoughtful, and a helpful rule we use is the **48-hour rule**. Before a goal can be changed officially, they have to wait forty-eight hours from when they tell us they want to change it (officially). Usually this happens because they're tired of waiting for the "bigger" goal and want to settle for something less. This protects kids from impulse without locking them into frustration.

It's always interesting to see what our kids choose to save for. In these early stages, I try not to debate their goals. What matters most right now is not *what* they are saving for, but that they are saving at all.

When children are given freedom to choose their goals, saving no longer feels controlled or imposed; it becomes personal. That sense of ownership fosters independence and helps the habit take root without turning it into a power struggle.

And, honestly, I've learned a great deal about my kids through this process. Especially with my teenager, the things he chooses to save for are often not what I would have expected. Paying attention to those choices has given me a clearer window into his interests, motivations, and heart—and watching that unfold has been both eye-opening and humbling.

In addition, when our kids get close to finishing one of their savings goals, we do not intervene and help them finish it. This is, in my opinion, super important. If our children have saved $32, and they need $35 to buy that LEGO set or whatever, we do not chip in $3. We let that delay provide its painful final lap.

Now, if they save $35 and we get to Target and show up at the cash register and it's $36 with tax, no problem. I'll chip in a dollar. But, at large, if they know there's a gap to complete still, we make sure they have the experience to complete it without us intervening. Also, money can flow from spending into saving, but not back. Once it is in the savings envelope, it stays there.

Giving

Our kids are setting aside 10 percent of what they earn for giving. It's not a lot, but it does add up over time and is a regular reminder that we are invited to share with those in need from the money we earn from working.

Giving should be personal, meaningful, and celebrated—not rushed or minimized. Whether giving to church, a cause, or someone they know, kids should feel the weight and joy of generosity. We try to make sure our kids have a personal connection and make the gift themselves whenever possible. This one can turn into a "Here, Mom/Dad, give my money to the church." We avoid that. If they want to give it to the church, they prepare the envelope with their information and turn it in themselves.

Even better, when they hear of or discover an opportunity that means something to them personally, those are special moments. Sometimes it means we need to give their money online (if there isn't a cash option). Then, we convert their cash to their Greenlight card, and let them process that gift online with their card information.

Again, the principle is making it personal.

Investing

Investing should be introduced slowly—almost casually—using companies your kids already recognize. The goal in the early stages is not technical sophistication; it is conceptual clarity.

Start with ownership.

If they drink Coca-Cola, buy shoes from Nike, or watch movies on Amazon Prime Video, you can explain investing this way: "When we buy a share, we are buying a tiny piece of this company. If the company does well, we do well." That framing is concrete. It connects investing to the real economy they see every day.

At this stage, keep comparisons simple:

- Saving is storing money.
- Spending is using money.
- Giving is releasing money.
- Investing is putting money to work.

You are building mental categories, not running a finance seminar.

Over time, you can layer in diversification naturally after they've seen their stocks go up and down—along with their heart! That gives way to a great conversation about investing in a broader basket of companies by using a mutual fund or an ETF as a means of reducing risk while retaining growth.

You can introduce the idea of index funds as simply "owning a little bit of almost everything," without immediately diving into expense ratios. The mechanics can wait. The mental model comes first.

Two guardrails matter in this chapter of the conversation:

1. **Avoid turning investing into entertainment.** Children do not need to experience investing as speculation. If it feels like a game or a scoreboard, you are unintentionally training volatility addiction rather than patience.
2. **Emphasize time more than return.** The most important variable in investing is duration. Show them how growth compounds—not dramatically overnight, but quietly over years. Investing becomes less about "winning" and more about consistency.

And most importantly, it teaches children that wealth is rarely built through dramatic moves. It is built through steady, disciplined participation over long periods of time.

Introduced slowly, investing does not inflate ego or spark greed. It matures perspective. It helps children see that money can serve something larger than immediate desire—and that they can learn to manage it thoughtfully.

Side Note on Greenlight

All our kids have a Greenlight once they turn seven, generally. The younger ones don't use it much and prefer envelopes. However, there are times that it is way better for them to have Greenlight loaded with their account balance than to be carrying cash. It's easy to swap out cash and put it onto their Greenlight.

For example, Max likes to buy items in Minecraft every so often (usually on a day off from school if he has extra screen time). We have HIS Greenlight card loaded onto the Nintendo account. He can spend what is there in Spending if he wants.

Or, if they are shopping for something online that they are saving for, let them put in their Greenlight. They feel so outrageously cool.

Anyway, point of the story: Greenlight is handy even if it's not used as a primary tool for allocating at younger ages.

When Not to Allocate: Exceptions That Matter

There are times when it makes sense not to require allocation. Usually, it's when they receive cash for birthdays or Christmas. We don't make them allocate that. They certainly can, and sometimes they do (because of the savings goal). But in our minds, that cash wouldn't have been allocated if it was given as a gift. So we treat it similarly in that regard.

Parents as the Bank—and Why That Role Matters

Throughout all systems, parents act as the bank and cash register. This role is not about control; it is about relationship and guidance.

Being the bank allows parents to

- help reconcile accounts monthly;
- notice patterns;
- ask questions; and
- celebrate progress.

Over time, kids internalize these practices and need less support. However, a good bank has cash and change readily available.

There's nothing quite like breaking down a $5 chore when your split is 50/40/10. Better have quarters on hand!

We will usually go get $50 of $1's and $5's every couple months. Often kids will trade in their cash to put it on Greenlight for something to buy online or otherwise, and so we get cash back more often than we expect.

Modeling Matters More Than Mechanics

Children are always watching. They notice whether parents allocate their own money. They see whether parents save, give, and say no. They absorb tone more than technique. Allocation in the home works best when kids know their parents practice the same principles at a different scale.

Showing your kids how you "say no" to things all the time is really eye-opening to them. It tells them you can "want" something, not have it, and be okay with it. "We have a budget. We didn't budget for that." Or, "That would be cool to have, but we are not less happy because we don't have it. We are glad for what we have."

Using language that reinforces contentment, gladness, gratitude, and perspective goes a long way with kids. They internalize the way you talk about money in ways we wouldn't expect.

The Long View

When children learn to divide money before they spend it, they learn to pause before they decide. That pause—practiced again and again across childhood—becomes one of the most formative habits we can give them. It creates space between impulse and action, desire and decision.

The next step is helping children understand *why* these systems matter—how money works, how choices compound, and how stewardship connects today's decisions to tomorrow's outcomes. That is the work of financial literacy, and it is where we turn next.

Key Takeaways

Before children can learn how to budget, invest, or plan long-term, they should first learn how to **allocate what they earn**. Allocation trains delayed gratification, self-control, and stewardship—skills that shape far more than money.

Basic Principles

1. **Earning changes everything.**
    - Money introduces both opportunity and risk.
    - Without structure, money trains impulse.
    - With structure, money trains restraint.
2. **Allocation matters more than amount.**
    - How money is handled matters far more than how much is earned.
    - Small amounts, handled well, form better habits than large amounts handled poorly.
3. **Allocation is part 1 of financial literacy.**
    - Before budgeting or investing, kids should learn to divide money intentionally.
    - Allocation teaches trade-offs, patience, and future-oriented thinking.
4. **Money is powerful—and needs guardrails.**
    - Like electricity, money must be governed to be useful.
    - Allocation acts as an "electrical panel," directing money safely rather than letting it run unchecked.
5. **Delayed gratification is the real gift.**
    - Learning to wait, save, and plan builds self-regulation.

- These skills predict long-term health, stability, and decision-making.
- Delayed gratification is formed through systems, not lectures.

Practical Practices to Implement

1. **Allocate the same day money is earned.**
    - Pay kids promptly.
    - Divide money into categories immediately.
    - Don't delay; connection between effort and intention is strongest right away.
2. **Use simple allocation categories.**
    - Spending.
    - Saving.
    - Giving.
    - (Eventually) Investing.
3. **Percentages matter less than consistency.**
    - Start with a simple split that fits your family.
    - The habit of dividing money every time matters more than "perfect" ratios.
4. **Let kids spend their spending money.**
    - Regret teaches better than lectures.
    - Freedom within limits builds wisdom.
    - Avoid rescuing or over-coaching.
5. **Protect savings from impulse.**
    - Allow money to move from spending → saving.
    - Do not allow money to move from saving → spending.
    - Use waiting periods (like a 48-hour rule) to slow impulse.
6. **Do not help kids "finish" savings goals.**
    - Let them complete the final stretch themselves.
    - The delay is formative.
    - Relief after waiting reinforces the value of saving.
7. **Make giving personal.**
    - Encourage kids to choose where and how to give.
    - Let them deliver gifts themselves when possible.
    - Celebrate generosity without rushing it.

Choosing an Allocation System

1. **Physical systems** (jars, envelopes, boxes)
   - Best for younger kids
   - Visible, tactile, slow spending naturally
2. **Transitional systems** (envelopes with oversight)
   - Teach planning and restraint
   - Introduce one-way movement (spending → saving only)
3. **Digital systems** (e.g., Greenlight)
   - Useful for older kids and teens
   - Reinforce allocation digitally with guardrails
   - Let natural consequences do the teaching

Role of Parents

1. **Parents act as the bank.**
   - Help make change.
   - Reconcile balances.
   - Ask questions and notice patterns.
   - Stay involved without controlling.
2. **Model matters more than mechanics.**
   - Kids watch how parents handle money.
   - Contentment, restraint, and gratitude are caught, not taught.
   - Use language that reflects stewardship, not scarcity.

Chapter 13

Financial Literacy—Part 2: The Power of a Money Script

Systems give our kids structure that develops good habits. Financial literacy gives them understanding for life.

By the time a child reaches this stage of the journey—work, earning, and allocating—they already know more about money than most adults realize. They have felt the tension of saving. They have experienced the regret of impulsive spending. They have watched money grow slowly and disappear quickly. They have participated in generosity and discovered that giving feels different from buying.

What they need next is not more rules. They need language. They need context. They need help connecting the dots. This is where financial literacy comes in.

Literacy Is Not About Mastery—It's About Familiarity

When many parents hear the phrase *financial literacy*, they immediately think of complexity: budgets, spreadsheets, compound interest formulas, or adult-level financial decisions. That assumption alone causes many families to opt out.

- "I'm not good with money."
- "I don't feel qualified."
- "I don't want to mess them up."

But financial literacy for children is not about mastery. It is about exposure. Many parents don't move into this space because they don't feel like they're winning with money. But this is not about you feeling good about how you're doing with money. This is about helping your kids develop the gridwork so they can understand better how money works and how the world runs. And this in no way needs to be complicated.

It is about helping kids slowly become familiar with

- the language of money;
- the flow of money and where it comes from;
- the relationship between work, time, and reward; and
- how money can work for them—or against them.

A child does not need to understand inflation at age eight. But they *can* understand that prices tend to go up over time—and before long, they'll start noticing it for themselves.

They do not need to grasp mortgage amortization at ten. But they *can* understand that homes cost money over time, and that most homes are purchased by borrowing money from a bank after a down payment is made.

They do not need to comprehend retirement accounts at twelve. But they *can* understand that starting early matters, and that money often grows significantly over long periods of time. Literacy is cumulative. It grows quietly through repetition, curiosity, and conversation.

The Hidden Problem of Invisible Money

One of the greatest challenges facing modern families is not ignorance; it is invisibility. Money used to be tangible. We wrote checks. We withdrew cash. We balanced registers. Kids saw money move. They carried cash or checks to pay for sports jerseys or registrations.

Today, money is silent and hidden. We insert cards, tap phones, Venmo pay, autopay bills. Money moves quietly and conveniently behind the scenes, often giving the impression that it doesn't exist at all. Until kids want something, of course—then we say, "Do you think money grows on trees?" And our kids think, *Well, no. Why would it need to grow on trees? It's all there on your phone!*

Children grow up surrounded by consumption without seeing cost. They experience benefits without context. If we do not narrate what is happening, our kids will fill in the gaps themselves—often with unhealthy assumptions.

The Statistics

It is not surprising that despite unprecedented access to information, financial literacy among young people remains alarmingly weak. Nearly half of U.S. young adults cannot clearly explain the difference between a debit card and a credit card.[49] Approximately one in four early adolescents do not understand that an ATM is directly connected to a personal bank account. Access has increased. Understanding has not.

Even with financial apps, digital payment platforms, and endless online resources at their fingertips, measurable gains in youth financial literacy have largely stalled—and in some cases declined. And the issue does not begin with children.

A significant percentage of U.S. adults struggle with foundational financial concepts such as compound interest, debt structure, and basic budgeting. Many parents feel unprepared to teach principles they themselves were never taught with clarity or confidence.

Money Scripts: The Stories That Shape a Lifetime

Researchers use the term *money script* to describe the deeply embedded, often unconscious beliefs people carry about money—beliefs formed early in life that quietly guide adult financial behavior.

Money scripts answer foundational questions long before we realize we are asking them:

- Is money a source of safety—or stress?
- Is it scarce—or sufficient?
- Does it create security—or fear?
- Is it private—or open for discussion?
- Is it a tool to steward—or a measure of identity?

These beliefs are rarely formed through formal instruction. They are absorbed through lived experience. Children do not internalize lectures nearly as much as they internalize atmosphere. What they observe becomes what they normalize.

If children witness panic around money, they internalize anxiety. If they experience secrecy, they learn avoidance. If they observe generosity, they learn trust. If they see restraint practiced with peace, they learn contentment.

Long before a child understands interest rates or investing, they are already forming a framework for how money feels—and that framework will shape decisions for decades. Financial literacy, at its best, helps parents become aware of the scripts they are writing—often unintentionally—and gives them the chance to shape those scripts with intention. When parents don't provide interpretation, kids still draw conclusions. They just do it alone.

Conversation restores visibility. It helps kids see that money comes from work, that work serves others, that choices involve trade-offs, and that limits are not signs of failure but signals of wisdom.

Conversations: How Financial Literacy Comes to Life

Financial literacy comes alive through **conversation**. Not formal sit-down lessons. Not "the talk." But short, frequent, ordinary conversations that happen as life unfolds—at the gas pump, in the grocery store, when something breaks, or when a want bumps up against a limit.

These conversations connect the dots. That's the best part of this exercise; it requires little effort on our part. In investment terms, this time has fantastic ROI. If work and allocation are the skeleton, conversation is what puts flesh on the bones. It's where aha moments happen—not because we planned them, but because we noticed them.

Talking "As You Go" Instead of Teaching "All at Once"

One of the most freeing realizations for parents is this: **You don't need to explain everything now**. Financial literacy grows the same way language grows—through repeated exposure in context. A few sentences here. A question answered there. Curiosity followed rather than forced. Some of the most formative conversations happen when we resist the urge to over-explain and simply narrate what we're already doing:

- "Let's watch the total go up while we pump gas. How many gallons do you think we'll hit? How much will it cost today?"
- "This bill for electricity is higher in the summer because we use more air conditioning."
- "We could buy that, but we're choosing not to so we can do something else later."
- "This broke, but it's okay. We planned for things like this."

These are small moments, but they carry weight because they are real.

Core Conversation Categories

Over time, kids should grow familiar with the *language of life*. Not mastery—familiarity.

Basic conversations often include

- what an ATM does
- the difference between debit and credit
- why gas, electricity, and water cost money
- needs versus wants
- why we don't buy everything we like
- how we save for unexpected emergencies
- why we don't buy things we can't afford

Intermediate conversations may include

- how parents budget
- why insurance exists
- what we save for
- what "rich" actually looks like (and what it doesn't)
- different personalities around money

More advanced conversations unfold naturally as kids mature:

- College costs and choices
- Careers and specializing in a field
- How big decisions are made
- Home ownership versus renting
- Investing and retirement
- How long-term planning works
- Why we say no to some good things

The goal is not covering every topic; it's staying open to the ones that surface naturally. It's to start giving them some gridwork. As you introduce words and language, kids will assimilate it slowly, and they will start noticing those things come up elsewhere.

We build some foundation, they begin to notice, and they start to assimilate patterns in life around money, work, decisions, status, etc.

What Years of Working with Money Has Taught Me

Working in finance has given me a front-row seat to how money actually works in people's lives. Over time, certain patterns repeat—patterns that often surprise people, including kids, but adults too.

These are some of the core lessons I regularly share with my own children.

1. Wealth rarely looks the way people expect.

Some of the most financially stable people (including millionaires) I've worked with over the years did not have extraordinary incomes. Teachers are a consistent example. They live within defined limits, contribute steadily to pensions or 403(b)s, resist lifestyle inflation, and build margin over time. The formula is not complicated: live modestly now, create freedom later.

The same pattern shows up among small business owners, skilled tradesmen, union workers, police officers, and long-term rental property owners. These are people who work steadily, understand the value of earned income, live within their means, avoid unnecessary liabilities, and save with intention. Over decades, that discipline compounds.

By contrast, outward signals of wealth are often misleading. Two brand-new vehicles in a driveway typically represents payments, not prosperity. What appears to be ownership is frequently leverage. Much of what looks impressive is simply financed.

Early in my career, the wealthiest client at one firm drove an old pickup truck coated in dirt, the tailgate secured with bungee cords. There was nothing about it that signaled affluence. Yet he had very substantial assets and virtually no debt.

Stories that flip expectations capture our kid's attention. When they discover that the "richest person in the room" might be the one driving the oldest truck, it disrupts the image culture they swim in every day. It reframes wealth as something quiet, steady, and earned—not flashy or loud.

2. Expensive things are often not owned at all.

The most expensive cars on the road are rarely owned outright—they're leased, borrowed, or financed heavily. The same is often true of large homes, cabins, or vacation homes. High cost does not equal high security.

This matters because children—and adults—are constantly forming assumptions based on appearances. Learning early that "looking rich" and "being financially free" are not the same thing is deeply clarifying. People who become wealthy don't usually feel the need to flaunt it. That's just been an observation of mine.

3. Money is a rival to God.

Over time, another truth becomes clear: Money does not create contentment; it reveals it. If fear is present, more money often enlarges it. If comparison is present, wealth can intensify it. Some of the wealthiest individuals I've known are also among the most restless—not because they lack resources, but because they feel they have more to protect and more to lose.

Financial growth and emotional peace do not automatically move together. We try to explain this plainly to our kids: more money does not solve problems in the heart. At best, it hides them for a while.

That is why we return regularly to conversations about money and allegiance, anchored in Scripture. Whether it is Paul warning Timothy about the love of money, Jesus confronting the Pharisees, the Sermon on the Mount, or the repeated counsel of Proverbs—it is everywhere. The sheer volume of biblical attention to money communicates something important: this is not a side issue.

We often frame it this way: Money is not evil. God gives people the ability to produce and steward it. But when money shifts from being a tool to being a treasure, it becomes a rival. As Jesus said in Matthew 6:24, "No one can serve two masters, for either he will hate the one and love the other, or else he will be loyal to the one and despise the other. You cannot serve God and mammon" (ESV). Money can serve good purposes. But it makes a poor master.

4. Working is good—and meaningful.

I've had jobs I genuinely enjoyed and others I simply endured. I'm honest about that with my kids because I want them to understand something important: The value of work isn't dependent on loving every moment of it.

When they ask, "Do you love your job?," there have been seasons when I've answered, "Not right now." But I always add what matters more: "I'm grateful to have work that provides for our family. Maybe someday I'll love it again. And if not, that's okay. Work is still good."

Spend time around people who are financially successful and you'll notice something interesting: they rarely talk about avoiding work. Many continue working long after they could stop. They understand that meaningful work shapes a person. It builds discipline, perseverance, humility, and responsibility. The goal was never simply to become rich, but to live a life marked by effort, contribution, and purpose.

Work will sometimes involve long hours, uncertainty, and fatigue. Not every effort succeeds the way we hope, and not every season feels rewarding. Yet the dignity of work does not depend on perfect outcomes. Faithfully applying our effort—building, serving, and contributing—reflects something good and God-given about human life. God values work, and we should too.

These conversations teach our kids that work is not merely about passion or compensation. It is about responsibility, provision, perseverance, and dignity. Work forms character—and approached rightly, it can also become a deep source of satisfaction and joy.

I remind my kids that many wealthy people value the journey as much as the wealth. That helps them see that the real value of work isn't just what it pays; it's what it builds in us.

5. It is healthy to enjoy what we already have.

Wanting newer or improved things isn't necessarily wrong. But the way we talk about what we want shapes the emotional habits of our home. When children regularly hear adults dwell on what's missing, what needs upgrading, or what would make life better, dissatisfaction slowly becomes normal. Over time, that posture spreads. Gratitude spreads just as easily.

In *True Riches*, Gregory Baumer writes, "Our faithful joy and contented spirit produce a ripple effect, the results of which we may never fully know. We look for results and influence here and now, but God is moving across nations and generations."[50] Stewardship, in other words, is not only about what we manage. It is also about the posture of our hearts.

Through my work with financial clients, I've seen how powerful that posture can be. Two people can have nearly identical levels of wealth and live entirely different emotional lives. One is content, generous, and grateful. The other feels perpetually behind—still chasing the next number, the next upgrade, the next sense of arrival. The difference is rarely the amount of money. It is the posture of the heart. One client can have "just enough" and abound in contentment, while another can have far more than enough and remain deeply dissatisfied.

Because of this, we try to be intentional with our language in our home. When the couch shows its age, the car is older but dependable, or our house is smaller than someone else's, we try not to complain—especially in front of our kids. Instead we say plainly, "We're grateful for what we have. A new car or bigger house might be nice, but it wouldn't make us happier. We're happy with what we have—and we're happy we have you."

We often assume kids love new things most. But what they value most is simply being present with their parents. They may not yet have the language to express that clearly, so they point to things that can be bought. In reality, a present parent matters far more than new stuff, and that kind of presence creates a home where children feel secure.

I saw this firsthand a few years ago. I bought an old GMC Sierra for a three-month renovation project. It cost $1,500, and my kids thought it was incredible. To this day they still talk about riding around the neighborhood together in the back of that old beater. A $100,000 truck wouldn't have made those rides any better. What made them meaningful wasn't the truck; it was doing something together.

Jesus also warns us about how easily our hearts can drift toward the things of this world. When he explains the Parable of the Sower in Mark 4, he identifies exactly what the thorns represent and what they do, and it is a sobering reality: "Now these are the ones sown among thorns; they are the ones who hear the word, and the cares of this world, the deceitfulness of riches, and the desires for other things entering in choked the word, and it becomes unfruitful" (Mark 4:18–19).

If we want God's word to take root in our children's hearts, we must teach them that the worries of life, the pursuit of wealth, and the constant desire for more will quietly crowd out what God is doing in us. I have often been struck by how someone with extraordinary wealth can still complain endlessly about what they do not have. In many ways, it resembles the same posture we see in spoiled children. Gratitude, on the other hand, reflects a heart that recognizes the goodness of what it has already been given.

The Deeper Lesson

Over time, these conversations teach a quiet but powerful truth: Contentment doesn't come from getting everything we want; contentment comes from recognizing that life is a journey of trade-offs, that having the best things won't make us happy, that moving the goal posts of desire will leave us empty, that truly wealthy people rarely flaunt it, that perpetually wanting more things will root out God's good work in our lives. When children hear these truths early, through repeated and honest conversation, they gain a kind of freedom many adults spend decades trying to recover.

The Power of Short Devotionals

Sometimes a good devotional time with kids is where these things click for them.

Just a couple weeks ago, during our usual family devotional, I was less prepared than normal. As we were moving toward the table to sit down, I felt drawn to Luke 16:10—the verse about being faithful with little and faithful with much.

There I was, sitting around the table with a fourteen-, ten-, eight-, and six-year-old. The entire reading and conversation lasted less than ten minutes—about the time it takes to finish an Italian ice cup. I literally buy Lindy's Italian Ice cups because it takes them around ten minutes to spoon through the ice. I shared a few examples of how we, as parents, try to be faithful with small things. We asked the kids what "little things" might look like in their own lives. We talked about what Jesus actually meant in context to the Scripture we were reading.

We talked about why it makes sense that someone who isn't faithful with little would struggle to be faithful with much. We asked if they could think of examples from their own experience—because I certainly could from mine. Some of the responses felt a bit surface-level. We prayed and wrapped up. The kids had stayed relatively engaged, finished their Lindy's cups, and we called it a win.

Later that evening, separately, without talking to each other—two of the kids came into my office at home. They were noticeably hesitant. Each had moved money from their "Give" envelope into spending recently and wanted to correct it. They brought the money back so they got the right bills and reset their envelopes properly. I hadn't known this had happened.

We talked briefly about it. I asked a few questions. This time, the idea seemed to connect. Because there was already a framework in place, and now a timely conversation, they could see why it mattered—not just financially, but spiritually.

What struck me most was this: They wanted to be trustworthy. With money, yes—but more than that, with God. They wanted to be faithful with what they had been given. That desire—to be trusted with little—was not something I forced or explained into them. It emerged through practice, structure, and a moment of clarity. And it was a gift to witness.

Wants, Needs, and the Gentle Power of "No"

One of the most formative conversations parents have with their kids is the one where they say no—and explain why. When kids hear us say no calmly, without frustration or guilt, they learn something essential: not getting everything we want does not diminish our happiness.

Walking through wants and needs together—especially in real settings like stores—helps kids develop discernment. Simply put, they will ask why. And you should be prepared with an answer. They are legitimately looking for understanding (most of the time).

Why? Because that's not a need. It's not in our budget. We already bought groceries with our budgeted money for the week. We chose to save money for a vacation, for a newer car, for your school clothes first—because it turns out if we bought a $5 item every day of the month for each of you, that would cost us hundreds of dollars that we have planned to spend elsewhere on things we want to do as a family.

I've been surprised how over time they fight back less. The most important thing is this: we say no all the time. Their happiness does not depend on a $7 pretzel at the concessions stand.

Calling one of their ideas "stupid," mocking a desire, or lecturing excessively about bad ideas or "wasting money" on things they are thinking about buying teaches kids to hide rather than ask. Curiosity thrives where interest and patience are present.

Parents don't need to approve of every want. They need to remain guides instead of judges. Let life provide the lesson. Let the system speak. Stay relational. Help them develop the habit; it has far greater returns than one-time decisions.

Again, we want our kids to feel freedom to ask us anything. If we give them framework for life and guidance as parents, life will teach them without it feeling so personal. And those conversations will build over time.

Why Financial Conversations Build Relationship

One of the most overlooked benefits of financial literacy is relational. When parents talk with their kids about money, something subtle but powerful happens: **kids feel trusted.** Money conversations invite children into the adult world. They quietly say, "You are capable of understanding how life works." That invitation builds dignity.

Shared Understanding Builds Trust

Parents often wonder what to talk about with their kids. We recycle the same conversations because it isn't obvious what else to say. Meanwhile, we're driving past a world full of opportunities—banks, businesses, job sites, water treatment facilities, power grids, new homes—that to our children feel like background props. But when we begin pulling back the curtain on how things work, kids perk up.

Because these are big-boy and big-girl conversations. How life works is exactly the kind of material that invites kids into deeper relationship, sparks imagination about the future, and gives them a healthier framework for thinking about their own lives.

Driving by a university, or a private school, or a community college . . . invites a conversation. Many of these conversations happen side-by-side—in the car, at a store, during errands—where defenses are lower and conversation flows more easily.

They create space for

- questions
- opinions
- disagreement
- curiosity
- shared problem-solving

All of which strengthen relationship.

Stewardship Is Discipleship in Disguise

When parents invite kids into financial decisions and explain their reasoning, they are modeling how to think—not just what to do. That modeling strengthens both competence and connection. Over time, kids don't just learn how money works. They learn how *you* work—what you value, what you prioritize, and how you navigate pressure and uncertainty. That knowledge builds relational safety.

The goal of financial literacy is not simply prepared kids. It is connected families. When kids understand how life works and feel invited into the process, they are less likely to feel entitled, anxious, or disconnected. They are more likely to feel grounded—and grounding strengthens (you guessed it) relationship.

In the end, the greatest gift financial literacy offers may not be competence at all, but closeness. And that is stewardship at its best.

Great Books to Spark Interest

As part of my teaching sessions, seminars, and workshops, I often bring a suitcase full of books—spreading twenty-five or thirty titles across a table for people to browse. Alongside other tools and resources, these books invite curiosity and conversation in a way few lectures can.

There is plenty of good content available, though I'll admit I always wish there were more—especially resources that help children engage money stories at a heart level, not just a technical one. Some of my favorite materials to read with kids are fictional stories that gently expose the emptiness of wealth when it becomes the goal and contrast it with the joy of contentment and generosity. These stories tend to linger long after the book is closed.

The Quiltmaker's Gift, by Jeff Brumbeau, for example, has a way of softening even the most stubborn hearts. It's the kind of story that can bring a tear to the eye—sometimes unexpectedly—and open the door to meaningful conversations about gratitude, generosity, and what truly satisfies.

Beyond that, we have some amazing resource that teach basics on topics like economics, which I think is more important for kids to begin understanding today than ever. Or, introducing kids to basic financial concepts like earning money, investing, saving for something significant, how stock markets work, what a rental property is, what a business owner is.

Months ago, after reading a book on money skills for kids, my ten-year-old came into my office a few days later and asked, "What is a business owner?"

What an interesting question! What we talked about next was super interesting to him. He didn't realize people just own stores, companies, or properties.

Elementary Years: Language and Curiosity

As kids grow, their curiosity naturally expands. This is when additional learning begins to matter—not as textbooks to be endured, but as conversation starters to be enjoyed.

The books below have been especially effective in our home. They're genuinely fun, and kids are surprisingly eager to learn about money—where it came from, how trade existed before currency, and why money changes in value over time. Conversations, for example, about inflation tend to stop them in their tracks.

"Wait . . . you mean the government can just print more money?"

That realization always leads to spirited discussion—and occasionally to the conclusion that maybe they should work for the government someday. We usually let that one sit for a moment before moving on.

For our younger kids, books like

- *The Quiltmakers Gift* (Jeff Brumbeau)
- *King Midas and the Golden Touch*
- *Money* (Joe Cribb)
- *Priceless Facts About Money* (Mellody Hobson)
- *Whatever Happened to Penny Candy?* (Richard J Maybury)
- *Money Skills for Kids* (Ferne Bowe)

These resources answer the questions kids are already asking:

- Where does money come from?
- Why do things cost what they cost?
- What did people use before money?
- How does money work?

The goal is not retention. It is familiarity.

Teens: Integration and Perspective

Teenagers are ready for synthesis. They are forming identity. They are comparing themselves to peers. They are imagining futures. This is where literacy must expand beyond *how* into *why*.

Resources like

- *The Money Challenge for Teens* (Art Rainer)
- *Money Skills for Teens* (Emily Carter)
- *Investing for Kids* (Dylin Redling)

These books help teens see that financial decisions are rarely isolated—they affect freedom, relationships, and options.

At this stage, conversations about college, careers, and trade-offs become especially powerful.

Parents: Other Books to Help in the Journey

These books and others are all listed and linked on my website:

- *Trusted* (Matt Bell)
- *Make Your Kid a Money Genius* (best non-Christian resource, by Beth Kobliner)
- *Smart Money, Smart Kids* (Rachel Cruz)
- *True Riches* (John Cortines, Gregory Baumer)

College as a Literacy Case Study—Not a Script

Thinking ahead about specialization—whether through college, a trade, or other advanced learning—is one of the most effective financial literacy tools available to parents. Not because every child should attend college or pursue a trade, but because these paths make *cost, value, and trade-offs* concrete in a way few other decisions do.

I'm careful not to frame college as the automatic next step after high school, although I do talk about it as something that is super normal. Instead, I treat it as a placeholder for a larger conversation about specialization. After high school, the real task is not extending adolescence, but discovering where a child's interests, abilities, and energy can be focused in a way that leads to meaningful work and a sustainable income.

I'm explicit with my kids about this: *The path to work you enjoy and that pays reasonably well usually involves becoming very good at something specific.* That specialization might happen through college, a trade, apprenticeships, certifications, or other forms of focused training. The role of education, then, is not to provide an experience, but to prepare you to explore and eventually commit to a career direction.

Seen this way, college becomes an investment decision rather than a rite of passage. That reframing changes the conversation. A few weeks ago, my high school freshmen mentioned an interest in attending the University of Minnesota. Great. We talked through why, what it costs, and how it might—or might not—align with areas he's interested in specializing in. As the conversation unfolded, he realized that choosing the U of MN was an expensive decision to make without knowing what he wanted to explore.

Instead, he became more open to alternatives, including starting at a community college, living at home, paying his way for a couple of years, and using those years to clarify direction before committing to higher costs.

What actually unfolds remains to be seen. But the shift matters. Post-high school options become about *discovery*, not about defaulting into a prolonged version of high school.

We try not to center these conversations around, "What are you going to do for the rest of your life?" That question carries more weight than most teenagers are equipped to hold. Although we do talk about things they enjoy doing and how they could eventually translate into a field of service. Instead, we frame it this way: "Over time, you'll have opportunities to grow in specific skills and explore different fields. As those interests become clearer, we can talk about next steps—college, trade school, apprenticeships, or other paths."

The emphasis is on development, not declaration. We want them to understand that career direction unfolds over time. Not a decision they make when they're fifteen years old. Because the goal is guidance, not anxiety. A child should not feel as though their entire future hinges on one early choice. The focus is steady growth, increasing clarity, and faithful effort—not premature certainty.

Walking through tuition differences, scholarships, loans, and expected earnings helps children see education as an investment rather than an entitlement. This isn't about burdening kids; **it's about inviting them into reality**.

If you plan to pay for your child's education in full, there's nothing wrong with that. It's a tremendous gift. But I would encourage you not to lead with that. Walk through the decisions together. Let them believe they have some skin in the game. If, later on, you decide to help pay off loans or absorb costs, you still can.

What matters most is not the funding decision itself, but the formation that happens along the way. When kids understand that education is tied to purpose, cost, and long-term trade-offs, they approach the future with far more clarity—and far less entitlement.

For full disclosure, the research I've seen does indicate that kids whose college is paid for (and they know it in advance) do graduate at higher rates from college. The downside is that they (on average) have lower GPAs, take longer to graduate, and transition into a career more slowly afterward than kids who were responsible for 50 percent or more of their education.

It's all about trade-offs.

Literacy Without Shame

One of the most important principles running through this entire framework is simple: **Shame is a poor teacher**. It may produce short-term compliance, but it rarely produces lasting understanding. When children feel shamed, their focus shifts from learning to self-protection. Curiosity narrows. Reflection stops. Growth slows.

Mistakes, on the other hand, are not failures of formation; they are part of it. Regret can be instructive. Consequences can be clarifying. A poor spending decision, a rushed choice, or an impulsive moment often teaches more effectively than any warning given in advance. What matters most is not that children avoid mistakes, but that they are given space to *process* them honestly.

This requires a shift in how parents respond. When parents stay curious—asking questions instead of delivering verdicts—children remain engaged. Questions like "What were you hoping would happen?" or "How did that turn out compared to what you expected?" invite reflection without defensiveness. They keep the focus on learning rather than blame.

A shame-free approach does not mean an absence of standards or consequences. It means that consequences are framed as feedback, not judgment. Children are still held accountable, but they are not labeled by their choices. Over time, this teaches them something critical: Mistakes are not threats to belonging, and growth does not require hiding.

Financial literacy, in particular, benefits from this posture. Money decisions are emotionally charged, even for adults. When children learn that they can talk openly about missteps without fear of humiliation, they become more thoughtful, more honest, and more willing to take responsibility. Freedom, paired with structure, invites growth in ways shame never can.

Modeling: The Literacy They Cannot Ignore

Perhaps the most powerful form of financial literacy is what children see modeled. They notice

- whether parents budget
- whether parents argue about money
- whether parents panic at expenses
- whether parents say no to themselves
- whether parents give generously
- whether parents are content

Children don't need perfect parents. They need **visible** ones.

Your example with money will be as useful as everything else you do with your kids combined. Because you become the source of example to them, usually subconsciously, about how money works.

We went through a hard time financially during the elementary years of our firstborn - and we can tell he has a different posture toward money than the other kids. He picked up on that stress and that unpredictable season differently, even though it wasn't talked about out loud in front of him.

How we handle money in front of our kids carries more weight than we often realize. After learning about how money scripts form, I've been intentional about what our children see modeled in our home. I want them to see confidence in God, ownership of our financial decisions, and clarity around why we say no to certain things.

Most importantly, I want them to know that Ashley and I are genuinely happy with what we have—even if it's less than what some other families enjoy. When children see contentment paired with purpose, they learn that money is something to be stewarded thoughtfully, not chased anxiously.

We love what we have, and having more stuff doesn't make us more happy. Anyway, that's been a journey.

Why Literacy Ultimately Points Beyond Money

At its deepest level, financial literacy is not about producing financially successful adults. It is about producing free ones.

Free from panic.

Free from comparison.

Free from consumption as identity.

Money is a powerful servant and a terrible master. When kids understand its limits, they are less likely to worship it—and more likely to use it well. This is where literacy becomes spiritual formation. Not because we preach at kids, but because we help them see money for what it is—and what it is not.

Some Is Caught. Some Is Taught.

This chapter rests on a few simple truths.

- Some lessons will come from books.
- Some from conversations.
- Some from regret.
- Some from watching you.

You will not get it all right. But if your kids work, earn, allocate, talk, and read—if they grow up with exposure, language, and context—they will carry a realistic framework for how life works. That framework is a gift. And it is one of the most loving forms of stewardship a parent can offer.

In Conclusion

Financial literacy is not about producing financially sophisticated children; it is about forming wise, free, and grounded adults through steady exposure, conversation, modeling, and relational trust. Systems build habits. Conversation builds understanding. Modeling builds belief. Some is caught; some is taught. A blend of ongoing conversations and reading books goes a long way.

---

15 Key Takeaways

1. **Literacy is familiarity, not mastery.**
    - The goal is language, context, and pattern recognition.
    - Understanding grows cumulatively through small conversations.
    - Parents don't need expertise—just visibility and consistency.
    - Literacy builds "gridwork" so life makes sense.
2. **Invisible money requires intentional narration.**
    - Modern money is silent (tap, swipe, autopay).
    - Kids see consumption without seeing cost.
    - If we don't narrate, they fill gaps with assumptions.
    - Visibility restores reality: work → income → allocation → trade-offs.
3. **Money scripts are formed by atmosphere.**
    - Kids absorb beliefs about money long before they understand it.
    - They internalize tone, stress, secrecy, generosity, and restraint.
    - What parents model becomes what children normalize.
    - Conversation gives interpretation to what they observe.
4. **Conversation is the engine of literacy.**
    - Not formal lessons—short, frequent, real-time conversations.
    - "As you go" beats "all at once."
    - Small moments (gas pump, grocery store, broken appliance) carry weight.
    - The ROI on everyday conversation is enormous.
5. **Core lessons come from real financial life.**
    - Wealth rarely looks flashy.
    - Stability is often quiet.
    - High income ≠ financial freedom.
    - Appearances are often leveraged, not owned.
6. **Expensive things are often financed.**
    - "Looking rich" and "being free" are not the same.
    - Security is built slowly, not displayed loudly.

7. **Money reveals the heart.**
    - More money magnifies what's already there.
    - Contentment is a posture, not a threshold.
    - Money is a tool—never a master.
8. **Work is meaningful—even when imperfect.**
    - Dignity comes from responsibility and perseverance.
    - Happiness is not postponed until ideal circumstances.
9. **Loving what we have shapes emotional climate.**
    - Gratitude spreads.
    - Complaint spreads.
    - Contentment creates relational security.
10. **Budget constraints reveal values.**
    - Saying no is about priorities, not scarcity.
    - Allocation reflects belief.
    - Limits teach discernment, not deprivation.
11. **"No" is formative.**
    - Calm, explained no's build resilience.
    - Shame shuts down learning.
    - Curiosity keeps relationship intact.
    - Structure + freedom produces growth.
12. **Financial literacy builds relationship.**
    - Money conversations invite kids into the adult world.
    - Shared understanding builds trust.
    - Literacy increases dignity.
    - The real win is connection, not competence.
13. **Specialization > pressure.**
    - Career conversations focus on development, not destiny.
    - Emphasis on skill-building and exploration.
    - College is an investment decision, not a script.
    - Guidance, not anxiety.
14. **Modeling is unavoidable.**
    - Kids notice everything.
    - Emotional tone around money matters deeply.
    - Visible contentment teaches more than instruction.
    - Some lessons are caught, not taught.

15. **The deeper aim: freedom. Financial literacy ultimately produces**
    - freedom from panic,
    - freedom from comparison
    - freedom from consumption as identity, and
    - freedom to steward wisely.

Part 3

Revealing Grace

Raising children in today's world requires more than good intentions; it requires clarity about the kind of people we hope they will become. The aim of this book has not been theory, but traction: practical ways to move a home from entitlement toward stewardship.

Along the way we have focused on areas like technology, shared work, and financial literacy—not because they are the only things that shape a child's life, but because they quietly influence how children understand privilege, responsibility, and gratitude.

Over time, these patterns create an environment where privilege is tied to responsibility and responsibility is guided by mercy. Children learn that effort matters, that limits are real, and that life requires participation. Also, kids who become grounded and grateful have the advantage of learning something even deeper: effort has dignity, yet it does not carry the day. Grace does. When responsibility and mercy exist together in a home, children begin to recognize grace in ways few other experiences can.

This short final section steps back and highlights that deeper idea—the ecosystem we've been building throughout the book and the role it plays in shaping a child's heart. From there, the final chapter will help you consider your next steps, offering practical ways to begin putting these ideas into motion and resources that can support you as you do.

With a little clarity, a little courage, and a commitment to responsibility over comfort, you can help your children grow into grateful, grounded stewards of the lives they've been given.

Chapter 14

From Entitlement to Stewardship

If you've made it this far, chances are you didn't pick up this book looking for theory; you were looking for traction. Many parents today feel like they're grasping for solutions, trying to reduce conflict, improve behavior, and preserve relationships while the pace and pressures of modern life keep accelerating. My hope throughout these pages has been to offer something practical and livable: a clear framework for raising grateful and grounded kids in an age of entitlement.

There are many aspects of a child's upbringing that matter deeply—education, spiritual formation, friendships, community, identity. All of those deserve care and attention. But the areas we've focused on here—**technology, chores and work, and financial literacy**—serve as anchors. They give families bearings. They reduce unnecessary conflict. They create shared expectations. And they help parents remain present and relational in a culture that constantly pulls children toward distraction, entitlement, and overstimulation.

This isn't about being at war with culture. Culture itself is not the enemy. But the dominant influences of the day—those that quietly shape desire, attention, and values—do require discernment. Every home has a culture, whether it is chosen intentionally or formed accidentally. When parents take responsibility for setting the tone and standards in their home, children get the opportunity to *feel* what grounding and gratitude are actually like.

They learn, through a clear and relatable household economy, how effort, responsibility, privilege, and freedom work together for their good and the good of the home. In effect, we are giving them the opportunity to develop an operating system in childhood that will serve them well in adulthood.

They learn that work carries dignity.

That self-control leads to freedom, not deprivation.

That responsibility is not punishment, but preparation.

That limits are an expression of love.

Over time, these experiences shape children into adults who are teachable, coachable, and capable—adults who still turn to their parents for wisdom when it's appropriate, because the relationship was protected rather than eroded. And if things go well—perhaps even into the next generation—these patterns are passed on.

It is a strange and rapidly changing time to raise kids. With the pace of technology and the emerging role of artificial intelligence, the pressure toward overstimulation and unmanaged desire is only increasing. Helping children experience a grounded childhood—with clear, loving boundaries around the things that most powerfully shape them—is not only for their good. It is also for the good of the world they will eventually help lead.

Privilege, Responsibility, and the Formation of Gratitude

One of the most important ideas woven throughout this book is simple, but far-reaching: **Privilege without responsibility leads to entitlement**.

But when privilege is *tied* to responsibility, it creates the conditions for gratitude to grow.

And as we've seen, entitlement is not something our children create on their own. That responsibility rests with us as parents. Entitlement does not happen by accident; it forms slowly through the environments, expectations, and accommodations we create, often with the best of intentions.

Gratitude is not something children decide to have because we tell them they should. It is rarely a choice. More often, it is a *perspective*—one that forms slowly through lived experience. Gratitude grows when children encounter effort, limitation, loss, and recovery. It grows when they begin to recognize the value of what they have because they have participated in sustaining it.

In other words, gratitude is not taught well through lectures. It is *earned* through formation. This is why chores, work, financial literacy, and technology boundaries matter so much. These practices introduce just enough friction into a child's life to create perspective. They invite children to wake up to the value of what they have instead of focusing on what they don't. They teach children—quietly—that good things are connected to effort, responsibility, and self-regulation.

When privileges are automatic, invisible, and never at risk, children come to expect them. What is expected cannot be appreciated. Over time, entitlement crowds out gratitude—not because children are selfish, but because they lack perspective.

But when privileges are earned, kept, and occasionally lost, something shifts.

Children begin to notice.

They begin to care.

They begin to feel ownership.

They begin to understand how life works.

And gratitude begins to take root—not as a moral obligation, but as a natural response.

Why This Matters for Relationship

Many parents hesitate to increase responsibility because they fear damaging the relationship. But what I've seen is that unmanaged privilege is far more corrosive to relationship than clear expectations ever are.

Entitlement quietly reorganizes relationships around consumption instead of mutual care. Parents become providers and referees. Children become negotiators and consumers. Resentment builds on both sides, even when love remains.

Responsibility, held with clarity and consistency, does the opposite. It steadies children. It reduces conflict. It removes parents from constant emotional arbitration. And over time, it preserves the very thing parents care most about: *future relationship.*

Children who grow up understanding responsibility are more likely to grow into adults who are teachable, coachable, and willing to seek counsel—not because they have to, but because trust was built and preserved.

Setting Culture at Home in a Complicated World

Today's cultural current pulls hard toward distraction, entitlement, comparison, and overstimulation. It takes intentional effort to resist that riptide—not with fear or isolation, but with clarity and structure.

When parents set culture in the home—through shared work, clear boundaries, and meaningful responsibility—children get to *experience* what grounding and gratitude feel like. They learn that work carries dignity, that self-control leads to joy, and that they have a role to play in the life of their family and community.

This is not about raising perfect children. It is about raising children who are prepared for real life.

The Foundation and the Structure

I originally set out to help parents disciple their children in financial literacy. What I discovered along the way was that our own home—and many others—needed something more fundamental before that work could truly take hold.

In practice, I came to see that **chores and technology plans form the foundation**. They uproot entitlement and create the conditions for belonging, responsibility, and self-regulation. That foundation matters no matter what you're trying to teach. Without shared responsibility and clear limits, homes struggle to function well—and children struggle to develop a sense of ownership over their lives.

Once that foundation is in place, however, my conviction about financial literacy has only grown stronger.

Teaching our kids how money actually works is more important today than it has ever been. The economic landscape they are entering will be less forgiving, more complex, and more uncertain than the one many of us grew up in. While new technologies—especially AI—will undoubtedly change how work looks, they will not eliminate the need for wisdom, discipline, planning, and stewardship. Predictions about effortless futures have been made before, and they consistently underestimate the realities of human desire, consumption, and responsibility.

However, until Christ returns, we will all still be called to work diligently, steward wisely, and live faithfully with what we've been given.

That's why I want to make one final encouragement: **Don't miss the window you have while your kids are still under your care**. The habits, assumptions, and skills they carry into adulthood will matter far more than any single prediction about the future. Financial literacy gives them clarity, resilience, and confidence in a world that will demand all three.

If you sense that your household finances lack structure—or you simply want a clearer, values-aligned plan that enables you to live well today while preparing responsibly for the future—I'd encourage you to look for a referral to a great financial advisor who shares your values. Talk to your friends and family about their recommendations, interview advisors, take your time, and make a good decision! There is not a one-size-fits-all, and there are many good advisors out there doing good work.

Toward Grace

When children learn to keep technology in its place, take responsibility in their shared space, and steward money wisely, they are not being formed away from grace; they are being prepared to recognize it. That's because grace is rarely noticed in seasons of comfort and convenience, but rather in seasons of challenge. Childhood provides many of these moments. In the challenges children encounter—temptation, responsibility, failure, and perseverance—they begin to discover both the limits of their own ability and the importance of how they respond.

In a healthy home, children begin to see how grace operates alongside privilege and responsibility. They learn that effort is within their control and that their effort matters. At the same time, they discover that our love as parents is not earned by getting everything right, because our goals aren't related to how they perform in life but rather who they become in life. Our love remains steady even when they fall short. In that contrast, something deeper becomes visible: Effort has dignity, but it is not the foundation of love or acceptance. It is the response.

When parents shepherd patiently in the home, with kindness and clarity, children begin to see a reflection of the same dynamic that exists in the Christian life. Effort matters, but it does not ultimately save, secure, or justify us. Instead, effort simply brings us to the place where grace becomes unmistakable. We come up short—and grace carries the day.

The idea that, in spite of all of our efforts, we are saved by grace becomes more accessible. As Scripture reminds us: "For it is by grace you have been saved, through faith—and this is not from yourselves, it is the gift of God—not by works, so that no one can boast" (Ephesians 2:8–9 NIV).

Grace does more than comfort; it confronts. Scripture tells us that "God's kindness is meant to lead you to repentance" (Romans 2:4 ESV). When children experience both responsibility and mercy—when they know what it costs to carry weight, and then receive forgiveness or provision they did not earn—grace draws them low, not in shame but in humility. It softens pride. It opens the heart. It makes repentance possible because love, not fear, is doing the work.

And it restores relationship.

This kind of formation matters far beyond the walls of our homes. We are raising children into a broken and polarized world—one marked by pride, tribalism, and relentless self-justification. What that world needs most is not louder arguments or stronger postures, but people shaped by grace. Grace produces people who are steady, humble, and free—people who can serve others without needing to prove themselves, and love without being ruled by fear or resentment.

When responsibility forms the soil and grace bears the fruit, children grow into adults who understand how life works—and how redemption works. They learn that effort has dignity, that limits are good, and that salvation is a gift. And over time, they are drawn back again and again to the heart of the gospel: *that while we labor faithfully, it is Christ who carries the weight we never could, and it is grace—given to us in Him—that makes us whole.*

As Paul reminds us, "I planted the seed, Apollos watered it, but God has been making it grow" (1 Corinthians 3:6 NIV).

That is not just good parenting. It is the quiet, faithful work of raising stewards—grateful, grounded people—who are prepared to love a weary world well.

Chapter 15

Next Steps for Traction

If you're feeling overwhelmed, unsure where to begin, or simply tired of trying to piece things together as you go, you're not alone. This book exists because so many families sense the same thing: *there has to be a better way*—one that is practical, relational, and sustainable over time.

That conviction is what shaped this work.

I don't believe families need more guilt, more noise, or more unrealistic ideals. What we need are clear frameworks, shared language, and the courage to lead with intention in a world that rarely slows down to help us do so. My hope is that this book has offered you clarity, not pressure—and a path forward that feels possible within the life you're already living.

Taking the Next Step

If you're ready to move from ideas to action, I've made additional resources available at www.RichRoadStewardship.com, including

- free templates for **technology plans**, **chores plans**, and other family systems
- curated reading and research-backed resources mentioned in the book
- practical tools you can begin using immediately in your home

You're also welcome to join my email list, where I share occasional insights, encouragement, and new resources designed to support families navigating these same challenges. No noise—just helpful content, shared thoughtfully.

Serving Families and Communities

I deeply value the opportunity to serve families—especially through churches, schools, parent groups, and community networks. Teaching in these settings brings the work to life, because conversation, questions, and shared reflection often lead to the most meaningful insight and change.

From the beginning, my aim has been to offer **short, focused sessions** that move people toward action without overwhelming them with details all at once. I still love that format. It creates space for clarity, momentum, and honest assessment. From there, families can decide whether they're ready to take the next step and engage more deeply.

Even when they don't, these sessions are designed to leave everyone with **practical takeaways** they can use immediately—without pressure or guilt. The goal is not to push people forward faster than they're ready, but to offer tools and perspective that serve them wherever they are.

Some of the formats that others have found to be most helpful include

One-Hour Sessions

Designed to be part teaching, part conversation. These are ideal for small or large groups, and typically focus on a single topic. They're a great entry point—practical, relational, and accessible—and often open the door to deeper engagement and clear immediate takeaways.

Seminars (1–3 hours)

More focused, topic-specific teaching with coordinated discussion and participation based on your group's dynamics. These work well for private schools, networks, pastoral gatherings, and learning communities.

Parenting Conferences for Churches

A start-to-finish, out-of-the-box experience grounded in raising grateful and grounded kids in an age of entitlement. These typically include an opening session, followed by a full day of teaching broken into core topics, with a workbook, breakout sessions, and opportunities for connection.

I'm open to other formats as well and enjoy collaborating to find what best serves your community.

Reach Out

I genuinely want to hear from you.

If you don't know where to start—reach out.

If you want help implementing what you've read—reach out.

If you want to introduce this work to a community that could benefit—reach out.

You can connect with me at www.RichRoadStewardship.com or email me directly at doug@richroadstewardship.com.

This work began with concern for my own family. And every time I share it with others, my own clarity deepens. I'm still learning, still refining, and still committed to the long work of raising children well.

Endnotes

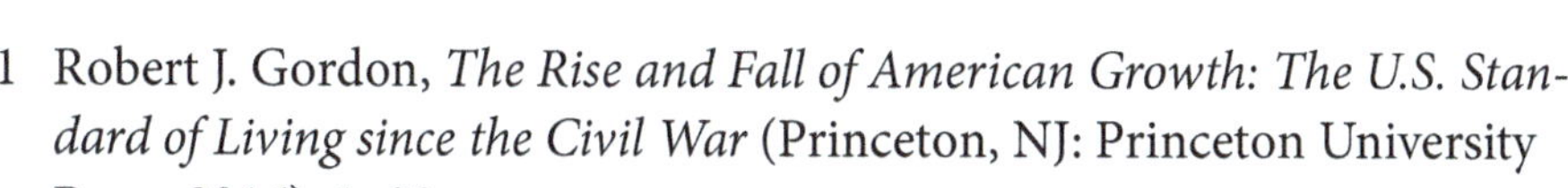

1 Robert J. Gordon, *The Rise and Fall of American Growth: The U.S. Standard of Living since the Civil War* (Princeton, NJ: Princeton University Press, 2016), 1–38.

2 Organisation for Economic Co-operation and Development (OECD), *How's Life? 2020: Measuring Well-being* (Paris: OECD Publishing, 2020), https://www.oecd.org/social/how-s-life-23089679.htm.

3 Ron Lieber, *The Opposite of Spoiled: Raising Kids Who Are Grounded, Generous, and Smart About Money* (New York: Harper, 2015), 10–11.

4 Beth Kobliner, *Make Your Kid A Money Genius (Even If You're Not): A Parents' Guide for Kids 3 to 23* (New York: Simon & Schuster, 2017), Kindle edition, loc. 707.

5 S. T. Hatidja et al., "The Effectiveness of Financial Literacy Education on Children's Economic Decision-Making: A Meta-Analysis," *Jurnal Obsesi: Journal of Early Childhood Education* 9, no. 1 (2025).

6 "Teaching Children About Money Now, Pays Dividends Later," *FDIC Consumer Resource Center*, September 2020, https://www.fdic.gov/consumer-resource-center/2020-09/teaching-children-about-money-now-pays-dividends-later.

7 Ashley B. LeBaron, Erin K. Holmes, Bryce L. Jorgensen, and Roy A. Bean, "Parental Financial Education During Childhood and Financial Behaviors of Emerging Adults," BYU Scholars Archive, 2020, https://www.fdic.gov/consumer-resource-center/2020-09/teaching-children-about-money-now-pays-dividends-later?utm).

8 TIAA Institute, *Financial Literacy and Retirement Fluency in America: Findings from the 2025 TIAA Institute-GFLEC Personal Finance Index*. 2025 report. https://www.tiaa.org/public/about-tiaa/news-press/press-releases/2025/06-09.

9 "The Average Age of First-Time U.S. Homebuyers Is 38, an All-Time High," *CNBC*, cited in the National Association of REALTORS®, November 5, 2024, https://www.nar.realtor/newsroom/in-the-news/the-average-age-of-first-time-u-s-homebuyers-is-38-an-all-time-high-cnbc.

10 Justin Whitmel Earley, *Habits of the Household* (Grand Rapids, MI: Zondervan, 2021), Kindle edition, loc. 403.

11 Erin Loechner, *The Opt-Out Family* (Grand Rapids, MI: Zondervan, 2019), Kindle edition, loc. 1593

12 Andy Crouch, *The TechWise Life: Everyday Steps for Putting Technology in Its Proper Place* (Grand Rapids, MI: Baker Books, 2022), Kindle edition, loc. 418.

13 Ibid., loc. 426.

14 Ibid., loc. 1411.

15 Loechner, *The Opt-Out Family*, Kindle edition, loc. 561.

16 Earley, *Habits of the Household*, Kindle edition, loc. 1383.

17 Ibid., loc. 440.

18 Ibid., loc. 2073.

19 Morgan Housel, *The Psychology of Money: Timeless Lessons on Wealth, Greed, and Happiness* (New York: Harriman House, 2020), 2.

20 Dallas Willard, *The Spirit of the Disciplines: Understanding How God Changes Lives* (New York: HarperOne, 1998), 5.

21 Dallas Willard, *The Great Omission: Reclaiming Jesus's Essential Teachings on Discipleship* (New York: HarperOne, 2006), 35.

22 Lieber, *The Opposite of Spoiled*, 3.

23 Maria Montessori, *The Absorbent Mind*, trans. Claude A. Claremont (New York: Holt, Rinehart and Winston, 1967), 186–193; and Maria Montessori, *The Discovery of the Child*, trans. M. Joseph Costelloe (New York: Ballantine Books, 1972), 80–88.

24 Geoffrey A. Fowler, "Algorithms Prey on You. What If You Could Reset Them?" The Washington Post, May 12, 2022, https://www.washingtonpost.com/technology/2022/05/12/instagram-algorithm/.

25 Loechner, *The Opt-Out Family*, Kindle edition, loc.144.

26 Jonathan Haidt, *The Anxious Generation: How the Great Rewiring of Childhood Is Causing an Epidemic of Mental Illness* (New York: Penguin Press, 2024), 216.

27 Loechner, *The Opt-Out Family*, Kindle edition, loc. 3221.
28 Molly Smith, "The Impacts of Social Media on Youth Self-Image," Loma Linda University Health News, May 16, 2023, https://news.llu.edu/health-wellness/impacts-social-media-youth-self-image.
29 M. Stephens et al., "Is Reading Contagious? Examining Parents' and Children's Reading Attitudes and Behaviors," Policy Brief no. 9 (December 2015), https://www.researchgate.net/publication/299346391_Is_reading_contagious_Examining_parents'_and_children's_reading_attitudes_and_behaviors.
30 Loechner, *The Opt-Out Family*, Kindle edition, loc. 824.
31 Adam Alter, I*rresistible: The Rise of Addictive Technology and the Business of Keeping Us Hooked* (New York: Penguin Press, 2017), 62.
32 David Tucker, *The Digital Parenting Guidebook: 7 Essential Steps for Building the Tech-Savvy Christian Family* (Cleveland, TN: Digitalparenting.com, 2024), Kindle ed., loc. 1369.
33 Loechner, *The Opt-Out Family*, Kindle edition, loc. 586.
34 Amy Orben, Andrew K. Przybylski, Sarah-Jayne Blakemore, and Rogier A. Kievit, "Windows of Developmental Sensitivity to Social Media," Nature Communications 13, no. 1 (2022), https://doi.org/10.1038/s41467-022-29296-3.
35 Siobhán Healy-Cullen et al., "Youth Encounters with Internet Pornography: A Survey of Youth, Caregiver, and Educator Perspectives," Sexuality & Culture 26, (2022): 491–513. doi:10.1007/s12119-021-09904-y.
36 Jinghui Zhang, Chenguang Dong, Ying Jiang, et al., "Parental Phubbing and Child Social-Emotional Adjustment: A Meta-Analysis of Studies Conducted in China," Psychology Research and Behavior Management 16 (2023): 4267–4285, https://pmc.ncbi.nlm.nih.gov/articles/PMC10591670.
37 Thorn, *Responding to Online Threats: Minors' Perspectives on Disclosing, Reporting, and Blocking* (Los Angeles: Thorn, May 2021), 18.
38 Ibid.
39 Ibid., 20.
40 Thorn, "Sextortion: Summary findings from a 2017 survey of 2,097 survivors," 2017, https://www.thorn.org/wp-content/uploads/2019/12/Sextortion_Wave2Report_121919.pdf.

41 Kristen A. Jenson, *Good Pictures Bad Pictures: Porn-Proofing Today's Young Kids* (Glen Cove, NY: Glen Cove Press, 2014).
42 Kobliner, *Make Your Kid A Money Genius (Even If You're Not)*, Kindle edition, loc. 541.
43 Marcus Buckingham and Curt Coffman, *First, Break All the Rules: What the World's Greatest Managers Do Differently* (New York: Simon & Schuster, 1999), 5.
44 Dave Ramsey and Rachel Cruze, *Smart Money, Smart Kids: Raising the Next Generation to Win with Money* (Brentwood, TN: Lampo Press, 2014), Kindle edition, loc. 336.
45 Kobliner, *Make Your Kid A Money Genius (Even If You're Not)*, Kindle edition, loc. 919.
46 Terrie E. Moffitt et al., "A Gradient of Childhood Self-Control Predicts Health, Wealth, and Public Safety," Proceedings of the National Academy of Sciences 108, no. 7 (2011): 2693–2698.
47 Angela L. Duckworth and Martin E. P. Seligman, "Self-Discipline Outdoes IQ in Predicting Academic Performance of Adolescents," Psychological Science 16, no. 12 (2005): 939–944; James J. Heckman, Jora Stixrud, and Sergio Urzua, "The Effects of Cognitive and Noncognitive Abilities on Labor Market Outcomes and Social Behavior," Journal of Labor Economics 24, no. 3 (2006): 411–482.
48 Celeste Kidd, Holly Palmeri, and Richard N. Aslin, "Rational Snacking: Young Children's Decision-Making on the Marshmallow Task Is Moderated by Beliefs about Environmental Reliability," Cognition 126, no. 1 (2013): 109–114.
49 EverFi, Millennials' Financial Literacy Study (Washington, DC: EverFi, 2019), https://everfi.com.
50 Gregory Baumer and John Cortines, *True Riches: What Jesus Really Said about Money and Your Heart* (Grand Rapids, MI: Zondervan, 2016), 45.

Resources

Gordon, Robert J. *The Rise and Fall of American Growth: The U.S. Standard of Living since the Civil War.* Princeton, NJ: Princeton University Press, 2016.

Organisation for Economic Co-operation and Development (OECD). *How's Life? 2020: Measuring Well-being.* Paris: OECD Publishing, 2020. https://www.oecd.org/social/how-s-life-23089679.htm

Twenge, Jean M. *iGen: Why Today's Super-Connected Kids Are Growing Up Less Rebellious, More Tolerant, Less Happy—and Completely Unprepared for Adulthood.* New York: Atria Books, 2017.

Twenge, Jean M., and W. Keith Campbell. *The Narcissism Epidemic: Living in the Age of Entitlement.* New York: Free Press, 2009.

Earley, Justin Whitmel. *The Habits of the Household: Practicing the Story of God in Everyday Family Rhythms.* Grand Rapids, MI: Zondervan, 2021.

Loechner, Erin. *The Opt-Out Family: How to Give Your Kids What Technology Can't.* Grand Rapids, MI: Zondervan, 2021.

Crouch, Andy. *The Tech Wise Life: Everyday Steps for Putting Technology in Its Proper Place.* Kindle edition. Grand Rapids, MI: Baker Books, 2022.

Lieber, Ron. *The Opposite of Spoiled: Raising Kids Who Are Grounded, Generous, and Smart About Money.* New York: Harper, 2015.

Housel, Morgan. *The Psychology of Money: Timeless Lessons on Wealth, Greed, and Happiness.* New York: Harriman House, 2020.

Willard, Dallas. *The Spirit of the Disciplines: Understanding How God Changes Lives.* New York: HarperOne, 1998.

Willard, Dallas. *The Great Omission: Reclaiming Jesus's Essential Teachings on Discipleship.* New York: HarperOne, 2006.

Montessori, Maria. *The Absorbent Mind.* Translated by Claude A. Claremont. New York: Holt, Rinehart and Winston, 1967.

Diamond, Adele. "Executive Functions." *Annual Review of Psychology* 64 (2013): 135–168.

Duckworth, Angela L., and Martin E. P. Seligman. "Self-Discipline Outdoes IQ in Predicting Academic Performance of Adolescents." *Psychological Science* 16, no. 12 (2005): 939–944.

Heckman, James J., Jora Stixrud, and Sergio Urzua. "The Effects of Cognitive and Noncognitive Abilities on Labor Market Outcomes and Social Behavior." *Journal of Labor Economics* 24, no. 3 (2006): 411–482.

Kidd, Celeste, Holly Palmeri, and Richard N. Aslin. "Rational Snacking: Young Children's Decision-Making on the Marshmallow Task Is Moderated by Beliefs about Environmental Reliability." *Cognition* 126, no. 1 (2013): 109–114.

Moffitt, Terrie E., et al. "A Gradient of Childhood Self-Control Predicts Health, Wealth, and Public Safety." *Proceedings of the National Academy of Sciences* 108, no. 7 (2011): 2693–2698.

Montessori, Maria. *The Discovery of the Child.* Translated by M. Joseph Costelloe. New York: Ballantine Books, 1972.

Tripp, Paul David. *Parenting: 14 Gospel Principles That Can Radically Change Your Family.* Greensboro, NC: Shepherd Press, 2016.

Haidt, Jonathan. *The Anxious Generation: How the Great Rewiring of Childhood Is Causing an Epidemic of Mental Illness.* New York: Penguin Press, 2024.

Siobhán Healy-Cullen et al. "Youth Encounters with Internet Pornography: A Survey of Youth, Caregiver, and Educator Perspectives," Sexuality & Culture 26, (2022): 491–513. doi:10.1007/s12119-021-09904-y.

Zhang, Jinghui, Chenguang Dong, Ying Jiang, et al. "Parental Phubbing and Child Social-Emotional Adjustment: A Meta-Analysis of Studies Conducted in China." Psychology Research and Behavior Management 16 (2023): 4267–4285. https://pmc.ncbi.nlm.nih.gov/articles/PMC10591670.

Thorn. *Responding to Online Threats: Minors' Perspectives on Disclosing, Reporting, and Blocking.* Los Angeles: Thorn, May 2021.

Jenson, Kristen A. *Good Pictures Bad Pictures: Porn-Proofing Today's Young Kids.* Glen Cove, NY: Glen Cove Press, 2014.

Ramsey, Dave, and Cruze, Rachel. *Smart Money, Smart Kids: Raising the Next Generation to Win with Money.* Lampo Press, 2014. Kindle edition.

Kobliner, Beth. *Make Your Kid a Money Genius (Before Graduating High School).* New York: Simon & Schuster, 2017.

Cortines, John, and Gregory Baumer. *True Riches: What Jesus Really Said About Money and Your Heart.* Nashville, TN: Thomas Nelson, 2020.

Buckingham, Marcus, and Curt Coffman. *First, Break All the Rules: What the World's Greatest Managers Do Differently.* New York: Simon & Schuster, 1999.

Smith, Molly. "The Impacts of Social Media on Youth Self-Image." *Loma Linda University Health News.* May 16, 2023. https://news.llu.edu/health-wellness/impacts-social-media-youth-self-image.

Fowler, Geoffrey A. 2022. "Algorithms Prey on You. What If You Could Reset Them?" Washington Post (May 12). www.washingtonpost.com/technology/2022/05/12/instagram-algorithm/.

National Association of REALTORS®. "The Average Age of First-Time U.S. Homebuyers Is 38, an All-Time High." *CNBC.* November 5, 2024. https://www.nar.realtor/newsroom/in-the-news/the-average-age-of-first-time-u-s-homebuyers-is-38-an-all-time-high-cnbc.

About the Author

DOUG GOODMUNDSON married his wife, Ashley, in 2007 and together they are raising three boys and a girl. Their home is best described as organized chaos, filled with hockey sticks, figure skates, and a ridiculous amount of laughter.

His passion for stewardship began in 2009 during his early years as a financial advisor, when he sensed a clear calling to deepen his understanding of Scripture's wisdom on finances. Over the years, teaching stewardship has become a central part of his life, spanning a wide range of topics. Today, his primary focus is stewardship within his own home—shaping family culture, parenting decisions, and priorities.

Over the years, his career has spanned both financial advising and nonprofit leadership, deepening his understanding of biblical stewardship in both theory and practice. Today, he serves as a financial advisor at Rich Road Financial, and as the director of Rich Road Stewardship, where he helps families develop a framework for stewardship in their homes.

With hundreds of hours of speaking experience, he loves helping people experience aha moments—making complex ideas clear, practical, and actionable. He enters every room with the goal of learning as much as he teaches.

He holds a BA in Economics from Saint Olaf College and an MA in Intercultural Leadership from Bethany Global University.

www.RichRoadStewardship.com

doug@richroadstewardship.com.

RichRoadStewardship.com

www.ingramcontent.com/pod-product-compliance
Lightning Source LLC
LaVergne TN
LVHW010654110826
845149LV00014B/3083

* 9 7 9 8 9 9 5 6 2 7 5 0 0 *

"George Bullard's previous book on congregational conflict was the best resource published for congregational conflict resolution, ministry, mediation, and management. I used it extensively as a primary textbook in teaching seminary courses, as a guidebook for mediating congregational conflicts, and as a handbook for training events and leadership summits. George's updated edition adds '*pure gold*' and groundbreaking insights on the impact of trauma, which makes *While Every Congregation Needs a Little Conflict* even stronger as the best of the best in this discipline."

—Reggie Ogea, director, Jim Henry Leadership Institute and Professor of Leadership and Pastoral Ministry, New Orleans Baptist Theological Seminary

"In George Bullard's refreshed classic, *While Every Congregation Needs a Little Conflict*, friction becomes your congregation's surprising engine for growth. Bullard offers a practical toolkit to address disagreements before they take hold of leaders and their congregations. This is an essential guide for any leader ready to turn difficult moments into significant breakthroughs."

—Tim Shapiro, author of *The Formative Power of Your Congregation and Divergent Church* and president, Center for Congregations, Indianapolis, Indiana

"George Bullard brings his remarkable experience with congregations to relevant application in the pages of *While Every Congregation Needs a Little Conflict*. Bullard's description of the seven intensities of conflict enables a congregational leader to accurately assess the degree of conflict. His discussion of leadership and processes for responding to conflict provides constructive responses. This two-step approach—assessment first, then action—is precisely what's needed in times of conflict."

—David Brubaker is an author, mediator, and consultant on change and conflict in religious organizations.

"*While Every Congregation Needs a Little Conflict* has a great plan for dealing with congregational conflict. George Bullard's understanding of what is needed in managing conflict exceeds anything I have ever read. It is tragic that such occurrences are part of real life. George provides helpful step-by-step approaches. Several decades ago, I was part of a congregation where he was the outside conflict manager. I ultimately made a personal decision to leave this congregation. Reading this book these years later, I highly recommend it to anyone trying to solve conflict in congregations and elsewhere."

—Ginny Britt co-founded Crisis Control Ministries and the Advocacy for the Poor in Winston-Salem, North Carolina, because all people are created equal and deserve assistance.

"George Bullard is an author of superb books on congregational life. *While Every Congregation Needs a Little Conflict* should be studied in every congregation and by every student preparing for Christian ministry. Why? First, George understands the radical changes in our culture impacting congregations. His attention to the reality of trauma is most helpful. Second, his seven intensities in congregations is a core part of the book and most helpful to those congregations in the highest levels of warfare. Finally, it is pleasantly readable. He has a style of writing that is clear without reaching for a dictionary."

—Larry L. McSwain is a retired college president and seminary professor who loves sitting in the sun with his wife in Arizona while enjoying their daughter's family.

"George Bullard provides congregations far more than a collection of good ideas. He offers a trustworthy guide shaped by the real pressures of congregational life. As a pastor, I encountered conflict at nearly every intensity George describes. Had I possessed this framework earlier, I would have approached these situations with greater wisdom and avoided unnecessary escalation. Now as a strategist for a fellowship of congregations, I can facilitate meaningful conversations with congregations. This book gives leaders a shared language, a healthy lens, and a redemptive pathway for engaging conflict. It will help congregations face reality honestly while moving forward to strengthen mission rather than fracturing the body."

—Chris Reinolds, mission strategist, Northeast Florida Family of Churches